TEACHING WITH ZOOM 2

AN ADVANCED USERS GUIDE

JOSÉ DOMINGO CRUZ

WAYZGOOSE PRESS

CONTENTS

PART 1
INTRODUCTION
1.1 What do I assume about you?   5
1.2 What kind of computer knowledge do I need?   7
1.3 What sort of equipment should I have?   9
1.4 What else do I need?   11

PART 2
SECURITY
2.1 What do you recommend for security settings   17
when scheduling classes?
2.2 What other Zoom security adjustments should I   20
consider?
2.3 Can you go over the "Security" menu?   23
2.4 What happens if I report a user in one of my   25
meetings?
2.5 What is two-factor authentication?   26
2.6 How do I set up two-factor authentication?   28
2.7 Should I use a password manager?   31
2.8 How can I use Remote Control?   33

PART 3
THE DIGITAL STAGE
3.1 Should audio be my top priority?   41
3.2 How important is my video?   43
3.3 What makes a good shot frame?   45
3.4 What should I take into consideration with   48
lighting?
3.5 How can I use virtual backgrounds more   50
effectively?
3.6 What else can I do with virtual backgrounds?   52

PART 4
THE EQUIPMENT ISSUE
4.1 How can I choose a good microphone?   57
4.2 Why do you recommend a lavalier microphone?   60

4.3 Should I get speakers or headphones?   62

4.4 What is that echo I sometimes hear in meetings?   63

4.5 What does the "Leave Computer Audio" menu item do?   65

4.6 How do I fix that crackling sound?   66

4.7 Why can't my students hear me play the guitar?   68

4.8 Should I upgrade my camera?   70

4.9 Do multiple monitors make Zoom easier?   72

4.10 Would a second computer be useful?   74

4.11 What other toys might I consider?   76

PART 5

ADDING TO YOUR ZOOM CLASSROOM SKILLS

5.1 Why don't my students turn on their cameras?   79

5.2 How can I encourage students to turn on their cameras?   82

5.3 How can I use the reactions at the bottom of the toolbar?   85

5.4 How can I make good use of the Raise Hand button?   88

5.5 How can my students see more of each other while I'm sharing?   90

5.6 How do I make the meeting toolbar stay visible?   93

5.7 Is there anything I should note about the "Mute" or "Stop Video" buttons?   95

5.8 What can I do for a class with students who are interrupting each other?   96

5.9 How can Zoom provide social outlets for students?   98

5.10 How should I best approach my Zoom problems?   100

PART 6

YOUR ZOOM WEBSITE SETTINGS

6.1 Customize Waiting Rooms   105

6.2 What meeting room settings do you recommend?   109

6.3 How can I get all those phone numbers to stop appearing in my invites?   112

6.4 How do I manage meeting functions?   113

6.5 How do I use templates?   115

PART 7

YOUR ZOOM APPLICATION SETTINGS

7.1 How do I access my App settings?	119
7.2 General	121
7.3 Video	123
7.4 Audio	125
7.5 Chat	126
7.6 Background & Filters	127
7.7 Recording	129
7.8 Profile	130
7.9 Statistics	132
7.10 Keyboard Shortcuts	133
7.11 Accessibility	134

PART 8

SCREEN SHARING

8.1 How can I make my Zoom windows visible during a screen share?	137
8.2 What can I use the iPhone sharing functions for?	139
8.3 Should I use the stereo or mono option for sharing sound?	141
8.4 What does "Optimize for video clip" do?	142
8.5 What does the green arrow next to the share button do?	144
8.6 Should I allow multiple users to screen share simultaneously?	145
8.7 What is the Vanishing Pen?	146
8.8 Why does my audience sometimes see blank spaces in my share?	148
8.9 Can I make the text in the shared browser window bigger?	150
8.10 How can I see more students while I'm sharing?	151
8.11 How can I make the image of the person sharing the screen bigger for a recording?	152
8.12 Why do my video recordings with shared screens have a vertical orientation?	153
8.13 What is the video sharing option like?	155
8.14 What do you use the "Computer Audio" option for?	156
8.15 How do I use the "Content from 2d camera" option?	157
8.16 How does "Slides as virtual background" work?	158
8.17 How should I use the "Portion of screen" option?	160

8.18 Can I share from my iPad? 162

8.19 Can I stop Zoom from resizing my window? 168

8.20 Can I make my slideshow not go fullscreen when I share? 169

PART 9

BREAKOUT ROOMS

9.1 How do I activate breakout rooms in my account? 173

9.2 Does Zoom allow users to self-select breakout rooms? 174

9.3 How do I rename Breakout Rooms? 176

9.4 Can users move between rooms? 178

9.5 Can I have students moved into breakout rooms as soon as I open them? 180

9.6 Is there a way to get better randomization of members in breakout rooms? 182

9.7 Are there better ways to communicate with students in breakout rooms? 183

9.8 Can I combine using Zoom with social media? 185

9.9 Can Zoom livestream to social media? 186

9.10 Do you have any other tips when using breakout rooms? 189

PART 10

ZOOM CHAT AND CHANNELS

10.1 How do I register contacts? 195

10.2 How do I make Channels? 197

10.3 How can I better use the in-meeting chatbox? 199

10.4 What's a faster way to respond privately if I'm in a large meeting? 201

10.5 Can I automatically have my meeting chats saved? 203

10.6 Should I allow my students to engage in private chat? 204

10.7 How do I make chat become a pop-out window? 205

10.8 Why does my chat become a pop-up window when I make my meeting full screen? 207

10.9 Can Zoom really do automatic speaker transcription now? 209

10.10 What are some alternatives to the Zoom whiteboard? 213

PART 11
POLLS

11.1 Are Zoom Polls still clunky and hard to use?   217
11.2 Why can't I find the Add Poll button?   219
11.3 How do I edit a poll after a meeting has started?   220
11.4 After a meeting/poll, how can I see the results?   223
11.5 How can I copy the Polls I made for one class to another class?   225

PART 12
ZOOM FOR OTHER EDUCATIONAL PURPOSES

12.1 How is Zoom used in academic conferences?   229
12.2 What is a conference "room host"?   231
12.3 How can I use Zoom's function for simultaneous interpretation?   233
12.4 How can I best use Zoom for pre-recording presentations?   236
12.5 How can I deliver a webinar?   240
12.6 How can I send large Zoom recordings to their destination?   243
12.7 How does Zoom fit into hybrid/hyflex classes?   245
12.8 What should I do about my microphone if I want to leave the desk in a hyflex class?   249
12.9 What's your other piece of advice for emergency hyflex classes?   252
12.10 What is Zoom like for social events?   254
12.11 Does Zoom have a registration system for special events?   258

PART 13
MISCELLANEOUS

13.1 What can I do to avoid Zoom fatigue?   263
13.2 Are you saying that Zoom fatigue isn't actually a thing?   266
13.3 Is there anything I should note about the View button?   269
13.4 What is Immersive View?   270
13.5 What's inside the green shield button in the top right corner?   274
13.6 What are the advantages of using a Learning Management System?   276

13.7 How can I improve accessibility in my Zoom classes?   278

13.8 External resources   282

Conclusion   285

Acknowledgments   287

PART 1

INTRODUCTION

It was March 13 here in Japan when I heard that the National Hockey League decided to postpone its 2020 season due to Covid-19 concerns. On April 7, Japan declared a State of Emergency in Fukuoka, where I live, and in seven other prefectures. Soon after, a State of Emergency was called across the entire country.

I first started hearing about Zoom in February, when one of my Facebook friends mentioned that she'd attended her first Zoom party. Soon news outlets around the world were reporting on how schools from K-12 to university were adopting Zoom as one of the software packages for teachers to use for these new conditions— what we all came to know as Emergency Remote Teaching (ERT). I soon started hearing the word *Zoom* often enough that I could see that what was happening in schools in Canada and elsewhere would eventually follow us here to Japan, just like the virus.

I realized I not only needed to know how to use the software for myself, but given my reputation as somewhat of a Macintosh geek, I might start getting calls and texts from friends and colleagues. To prepare myself, I started reading up on what the software could do.

Zoom seemed overwhelming at first, with all its features and buttons and settings designed to work as software for conferences and meetings. I had to learn like everyone else to adapt it to a classroom paradigm that at the time I knew practically nothing about: online learning.

But through force of will and my natural tendency to be curious about interesting software, I learned most of Zoom's capabilities. I soon found myself regarded as pretty good with the software by first my Facebook friends, then the people in Fukuoka JALT (Japan Association for Language Teaching), and then fatefully another Facebook group I had just joined called Online Teaching Japan. It was there that I got a nationwide reputation for being good at explaining what I know.

We collected and organized those things I learned for this second volume of *Teaching With Zoom*. I'm not trying to provide comprehensive coverage of every little detail. Much of what I have purposely not written about are things I consider to be at a beginner's level (for which, see *Teaching with Zoom 1: A Guide for Complete Beginners*) or not particularly relevant to teachers.

I focused on the questions that are often asked of me, the questions that I have asked myself, and the questions that I think many teachers would like to ask if they had the opportunity. I also wrote about some features that have changed substantially since volume 1 of this series was published.

If you find any features discussed here are not accessible or activated, check with your IT administrator and tell them the exact name of the feature you want to have turned on. If, as in my case, you work in a university that doesn't use English as its primary language, you'll need to know the name of the feature in the other language:

PRO TIP: Search the Zoom support pages for the explanation of the feature in your own language, then at the bottom of the support page you'll find the pop-up menu on the bottom right that will switch the language of that support page. Choose the target language, make sure you have the right information on the new page, and give that url to the IT admin of your school. Use the information on that page to learn the new vocabulary in the other language when you have to speak to the IT people.

1.1 WHAT DO I ASSUME ABOUT YOU?

You're probably like me, and you've spent the last year or two in a bit of flurry, trying to adjust to the new situation we found ourselves in. As part of that, teleconferencing software like Teams, Webex, and of course Zoom became a deep part of your teaching. You may have even bought the first book in this series.

Along the way you picked up some good lessons about distance teaching: things you know you should avoid, things you do well, things you want to try. You know enough about running Zoom that the terminology doesn't confuse you, you know how to do the basic tasks, and you can now concentrate a little less on the technology and more on teaching.

With this experience, you now find yourself wanting to sharpen your skills further and make yourself a better remote learning instructor. You feel that Zoom is your teleconferencing software of choice and want to get deeper explanations of what it can really do. You want to catch up with how it's evolved, but you haven't had time to fully explore on your own. Or perhaps you're relatively new to Zoom but not to remote teaching, so you don't need to have basic concepts explained to you, but you still need to learn how Zoom implements general functions in its own environment.

1.2 WHAT KIND OF COMPUTER KNOWLEDGE DO I NEED?

You might not be a computer expert, but you know your way around the software you use and don't often find yourself confused by what your computer seems to be doing. You might want some new equipment and accessories to extend your capabilities, and aren't afraid to stretch out and combine Zoom with other available software to help you conduct a better classroom. If somebody asked you to name your computer knowledge level, you'd probably say high beginner to low intermediate—or better.

You should also be clear that Zoom has two sets of settings controls for every account: one on their website and another in the application itself. The two can be confusing, so throughout this book I'll make sure to indicate when I am talking about website settings and when I'm referring to the application settings.

Above all, when you're making adjustments or trying new techniques or software, I suggest that as much as possible, try it out in a Zoom room first. See if the new microphone actually sounds OK by recording yourself solo. If you have a second device that can record, do the recording from there as well to further test the simulation. Does that new technique require too many mouse clicks from you? Does using that tablet and digital stylus actually work the way you imagined?

Another skill I suggest you develop is how to use your browser's text search function when you're looking around Zoom's account website settings. For example, if you heard recently that Zoom has a new feature for *closed captioning,* you could scroll up and down the website looking for the feature, perhaps passing over it a couple of times before you finally find it—hopefully before you give up in frustration. Instead, just press Command-F (PC: Control-F) on your keyboard and your browser will reveal its text search function. Then you can just type in the word you're looking for, and the browser will very quickly find it for you.

Learn how to use Zoom's support and resource pages. There's a wealth of information there with lots of example videos, and even a section on how to use the software in the classroom. You'll find them accessed as buttons on the very top right corner of Zoom's website when you log in.

1.3 WHAT SORT OF EQUIPMENT SHOULD I HAVE?

I don't want to ask you to spend any extra money on hardware or software unless it's necessary. At the time of this writing (May 2021), the newest version of Zoom is v5.6.1. You should have that downloaded and installed. You probably already have a desktop or notebook computer that you bought recently or only a few years ago that's in good shape. If that computer worked well for you before, there is no reason related to Zoom that you would need to go out and buy a new one.

If you do, however, choose to buy a new computer, get one a few weeks before you need to start teaching with it. You need time to move your files and applications and get everything ready for classes.

I strongly recommend that you have a professional-level account for Zoom that is paid for either by you or your teaching institution. The free version has a 40-minute limit on group calls and certain functions disabled, and that just puts too many restrictions on being able to run a class well. There are workarounds you can find on the web, but I don't think using them and then asking your students to cooperate is something you want to rely on week after week.

You need a strong and stable internet connection. You probably know by now that a wired LAN cable connection is always going to be more stable than using wifi from that same connection. If you're in the market for a new Ethernet cable, get one that's the shortest you can get away with for your setup. It should be rated category 6E or better. The higher the number, the better the quality of the cable. (Note though that higher cable numbers don't always mean faster connection speeds.)

1.4 WHAT ELSE DO I NEED?

You don't need any other specialized equipment like external microphones or web cameras, but good choices when buying such equipment will strongly enhance your Zoom presence, something we'll discuss throughout this book. Sections II The Digital Stage and III The Equipment Issue are the ones you'll want to read if you have an itch to buy extra toys.

We should also recognize that while pedagogy in the digital age has created a lot of new challenges, we shouldn't think of all problems from here as requiring brand-new solutions. In some cases, it takes just a flexible reworking of approaches that have worked in the past.

Communication with your peers and students becomes even more important when you can't all be in the same room. How we communicate is different, but the principles certainly won't change.

Critical thinking becomes especially crucial as you have to face all kinds of new problems to solve. It will take you miles in learning new software or hardware.

There are two soft skills, however, that were truly core to whatever success I experienced as I learned how to become a teacher in a remote digital context: **Compassion** for both your students and yourself; and seeking and participating in **Community.**

I saw myself get wrapped up in the whirlwind of everything that was happening as I got thrown into remote teaching with little support. It was a softer landing for me in some ways as most schools here in Japan deferred the start of semester after the virus made it onto the archipelago, giving me time to learn at least a few things that I needed to just get started with my classes.

But once the semester did start, I was overwhelmed with everything that made life so hard for teachers: unfamiliar settings, confusing directives, uncooperative tools, a burgeoning email inbox, etc. I'm not a calm and peaceful monk—I don't even meditate—but I did read enough of the works of Joseph Campbell to learn how important compassion can be to navigating difficult situations. A little self-forgiveness goes a long way; it helped me understand that what I was feeling was probably what my students were feeling, and that made me more capable of giving everyone the leeway they needed.

My instincts were confirmed by my participation in the online community **Online Teaching Japan,** a Facebook group that will now indelibly be a part of my teaching career. It was there that I found new friends who taught me much more than I had ever learned elsewhere: new ideas that I needed to succeed in the remote classroom; peers with whom I both agreed and disagreed; knowledge and chances to learn. I suggest you seek out your own community, or like the leader of OTJ, David Juteau, build one. There was no way I could have navigated remote teaching successfully without that community. I literally would not be writing this book if it weren't for my presence there and the opportunities I was given.

Find a cohort that you like working with and share your ideas.
Everybody needs friends.

PART 2

SECURITY

Zoom's reputation was taking hits back in the late spring of 2020 as numerous incidents surfaced regarding how it handled security, which caused entire organizations like certain American city and state governments and companies like SpaceX to ban its use.

In its early days, Zoom continued to shoot itself in the foot by making questionable policy decisions regarding requests by authoritarian regimes to deny targeted users access to their accounts, and to be misleading about the quality of its communications encryption, even as stories of Zoombombing made users worry.

I myself have been Zoombombed, but I think that Zoom has done an adequate job of addressing most of those earlier concerns. Organizations that once banned Zoom, like the New York City Public Schools system, are now back to allowing its use.

Not all the problems have gone, and I don't expect they all ever will, as some of them, like user ignorance for implementation or the nature of simple social engineering as the main vector for phishing attacks, are beyond the complete reach of Zoom's or any software's designers.

Most cases of Zoombombings have been perpetrated not by intruders but by participants who were actually scheduled to be part of a meeting—employees or students who were just suffering from pent-up stress and frustration.

Thus, while I encourage you to keep your security strong, you really don't have to be too fearful of outside intruders (especially if you follow my recommendations). This way you can concentrate more on creating a good teaching environment, where your class-room is not contributing to your students' anxiety.

For more information, see

https://www.proofpoint.com/us/security-awareness/post/ransomware-and-phishing-attacks-why-anti-virus-software-cant-save-you)

2.1 WHAT DO YOU RECOMMEND FOR SECURITY SETTINGS WHEN SCHEDULING CLASSES?

Around the fall of 2020, Zoom set new security standards when creating meetings as part of their effort to redress their damaged reputation from all the Zoombombings and other incidents I mentioned before. I think they did a good job in helping protect teachers and their classrooms without making their software much harder to use.

The first change they made is that Security is now its own heading and at the very top in the account website settings. The default though is that having minimum security requirements is set to **off**, as they wanted to make it optional for users to decide what level of security they want.

I recommend that you set higher levels of security to protect your classroom: slide that setting to the right and turn it on. The setting immediately below it for **Waiting Room** is already turned on by default. Keep it there. Keep the one below that for **Require a passcode when scheduling new meetings** set to **on** as well.

Security

Require that all meetings are secured with one security option

Require that all meetings are secured with one of the following security options: a passcode, Waiting Room, or "Only authenticated users can join meetings". If no security option is enabled, Zoom will secure all meetings with Waiting Room. Learn more v̄

Waiting Room

When participants join a meeting, place them in a waiting room and require the host to admit them individually. Enabling the waiting room automatically disables the setting for allowing participants to join before host.

Zoom's security settings

Now every time you set new meetings, the defaults will have waiting rooms and passcode as part of the settings. This is actually not such a big change from what you were probably already doing before the new security standards were put in, but now you're making it part of the defaults. You can always change the settings any time you make a new meeting.

PRO TIP: See the entry on customizing your waiting rooms. There you can explain the security requirements or give instructions on what to read in your syllabus so that students can reset their account settings and enter your room.

The third option that Zoom recommends is that only users who have logged into their accounts can join a meeting or a classroom. This one I still recommend, but you have to be careful how you implement it. If you turn this on, you might have some students unable to come in if they haven't created an account and logged in. Therefore, you have to make sure that students know how to get an account, how to install the software on their computer or mobile device, and how to login on either the website or their device.

PRO TIP: Meeting IDs are always Arabic numerals as per Zoom's system, as they wanted to make it just as easy for users joining by phone as by computer to enter a meeting ID or passcode. Entering a numeric code on a phone however requires one more button push to switch to the numbers on the phone keyboard, so I suggest making your passcodes with alphabet characters, unless you actually intend to have students join your entire class using audio only via voice call from their phone. Using Roman letters is just as secure, and makes it easier for users on mobile devices with keyboards to enter passwords.

With these three security measures—waiting room, passcodes for meetings, user authentication—you have pretty much protected your classroom from random intruders.

2.2 WHAT OTHER ZOOM SECURITY ADJUSTMENTS SHOULD I CONSIDER?

Zoom has great screen sharing features, but there are a couple of things you might want to consider. Take a look at how I have configured my account website settings.

By default, Zoom sets screen sharing to *host only* for both of the detailed settings. Some teachers are tempted to make it easier on themselves by setting that to **All participants**, but I advise against it.

As teachers, we will always encounter students who have never used Zoom before, and I've seen firsthand a meeting go a bit awry when someone who quite innocently started playing with buttons they were looking at for the first time accidentally shared the contents of their desktop. If you ever want to pass over screen sharing privileges to anyone during a meeting, it's easy enough with the in-meeting **Security** menu.

Screen sharing

Allow host and participants to share their screen or content during meetings

Who can share?

⦿ Host Only   ○ All Participants ⑦

Who can start sharing when someone else is sharing?

○ Host Only   All Participants ⑦

Disable desktop screen sharing for meetings you host

When this option is on, users can only share selected applications and files. ⟨v⟩

Annotation

Allow host and participants to use annotation tools to add information to shared screens ⟨v⟩

Security for screen sharing

Annotation can also be quite useful in small meetings or in classes that you know well, as it allows anyone to quickly add or edit on a shared screen; that's great for brainstorming and group work. Unfortunately, Zoom has the default set to **On**, and if you do end up with someone in your meeting who wants to misuse an otherwise perfectly good tool, this would be a prime opportunity. With **Annotation** set to **On**, they can take any screen share and scribble all sorts of things.

Annotations are controlled on your account's website setting—not surprisingly, under the heading **Annotations**. If you want to use annotation for certain points in a classroom, choose the second checkbox, **Only the user who is sharing can annotate.**

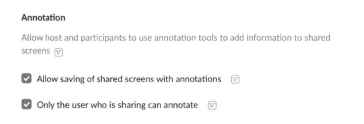

Annotation

Allow host and participants to use annotation tools to add information to shared screens 🔽

☑ Allow saving of shared screens with annotations 🔽

☑ Only the user who is sharing can annotate 🔽

To use annotations in class yourself

If you or whoever is sharing wishes to let others annotate on a particular occasion, just go to the **More** menu on the far right of the Sharing toolbar, click it, and look for **Enable Annotation for Others**. To turn off annotations after you're done, look for the menu item in the same location, but it will have the turned into **Disable Annotation**....

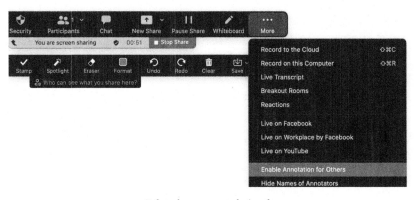

To let others annotate during class

While **Annotation** should be used with a bit of caution, you'll notice that my account is set to allow it. that's because I'm finding myself using Zoom's **Vanishing Pen** sometimes in my classes, something I discuss in section 8.7.

2.3 CAN YOU GO OVER THE "SECURITY" MENU?

Unlike the **Mute** or **Stop/Start Video** buttons, the **Security** icon is not a button in itself, but instead reveals the actions you can take during a meeting to help with security. Ever since the word "Zoombomb" entered the world lexicon, Zoom had been under pressure to take measures to reduce such incidents. For the most part they have responded, and while the software's security is not yet impregnable, it is much less vulnerable now.

WHAT DOES "LOCK MEETING" DO?

Checking this option will prevent anyone else from entering the meeting. If all of your designated members have already joined, you can lock the meeting, and anyone who tries to join will be told that the meeting is locked. You can unlock the meeting at any time.

WHY WOULD I WANT TO "HIDE PROFILE PICTURES"?

It might come in handy as an added measure to protect students in a large class from unwanted behavior; someone, say, clicking on the pictures of all the people s/he were interested in stalking. Some students' minds may be put at ease if this measure is combined with no requirement to have their cameras on.

WHAT DOES "SUSPEND PARTICIPANT ACTIVITIES" DO?

This is another feature of Zoom that I've happily never had to use, but if you're in a situation where an intruder or argument has created so much confusion that it's getting difficult to control the room, or you're having trouble finding the name of the individual you want to report and boot from the meeting, you can use this as a nuclear option to pause all the activity in the entire meeting to let you then take the next step, whether that be reporting the individual to Zoom or just calling his or her parents.

Suspending activity means all shared screens, all cameras and mics, and all chat will be paused. No one except you has control of these facilities until you lift the pause. I would suggest that you make sure that all your students know that you are taking this drastic measure before you do, or some might get confused about why their cameras and mics have stopped working and try to leave the meeting and rejoin.

Before you suspend the meeting, choose carefully whether or not you want to report the incident to Zoom. You might not want to do that if the problem was not clear-cut or might have been a misinterpretation on your part. Also be aware of any local laws or school policies that require you to report any kind of abuse, bullying, or harassment.

When you feel that you can safely restart the meeting, go to the **More** button at the bottom of the participants list, and in the bottom section of the popup menu that appears, you will find the items to check to allow students to unmute and restart their cameras.

2.4 WHAT HAPPENS IF I REPORT A USER IN ONE OF MY MEETINGS?

Then you'll have an experience that I have yet to claim. For the person you're reporting, probably nothing good, at least according to the warnings that appear in the **Report** box when you click the Report button. Not only will the user you select in the pop-up menu be thrown out of your meeting, but their account will be immediately reported to Zoom.

By default, only hosts and co-hosts are immediately allowed to report problem users, but if you want everyone in a meeting to have that option, you'll find that in your account's website settings (**Report to Zoom**). If it looks like you aren't able to use the **Report** button and can't access the switch to turn it on in your website settings, then contact your account administrator.

2.5 WHAT IS TWO-FACTOR AUTHENTICATION?

Now we need to talk about securing your account.

Basically, two-factor authentication (2FA) uses two login confirmations from different devices in combination to tell Zoom that you are who you really say you are. First will be the account passcode that you used to set up your Zoom account. Then when you set up 2FA, Zoom will send a text message to your chosen second device, most likely your smartphone, giving it a temporary code that you enter as the second authentication factor.

Now, even if someone steals your passcode, they would also need to have physical access to your phone to be able to get into your Zoom account.

PRO TIP: If you have any accounts that require you to login via a web browser and they're run by a good company that has the resources, they've probably already asked you to consider setting two-factor authentication to help secure your account. Apple does it, Google does it, any large IT company will have it available. Try to set it up on as many of your accounts as possible.

2.6 HOW DO I SET UP TWO-FACTOR AUTHENTICATION?

Go to the Zoom.us website and log in. On the left-hand side, look for the section labeled **Profile**, which is at the top. Click it, and near the bottom of the Profile page you'll find a setting for **Two-factor Authentication** (2FA). To the right side of it is a blue button, **Turn on**. Click that.

| Host Key | ******** Show | Edit |
| Two-factor Authentication | **Turned off** | Turn on |

Turn on 2-factor authentication

Next you'll be asked for the passcode for your Zoom account. Once you enter it, the dialogue box will disappear, and you might think you're done, but you're not. Look again in the same place and now the 2FA button has changed to **Turn Off**, and below it are choices for how you want to set up your 2FA.

Two-factor Authentication	On	Turn Off
	Authentication App	Not configured Set Up
	SMS	Not configured Set Up

Two-factor authentication options

You can do it either through an authentication app like Google Authenticator, or you can do it via SMS. An authentication app can be more secure. I use SMS myself as I find it simpler, and in the spirit of not asking my readers to obtain any unnecessary third-party software, I'll outline the SMS procedure here.

Click the **Set Up** button next to the SMS option. You'll be asked to enter your Zoom account passcode. Next you'll be asked to enter the country code for your phone number. If you don't know it, click the arrow at the right of the entry field and scroll to find your country. Then enter your cell (mobile) phone number with no spaces. If your number starts with a zero, you should probably not enter that first zero. You'll have to do one of those recaptcha puzzles where you have to click to identify three squares of bicycles or whatever.

If you're successful, Zoom will refresh the browser page to display an entry field for the six-digit 2FA code, then send it to your phone via SMS. Enter the six-digit code, and your setup is complete.

SMS Authentication Setup

Enter your phone number below. Zoom will use this phone number for authentication purposes only.

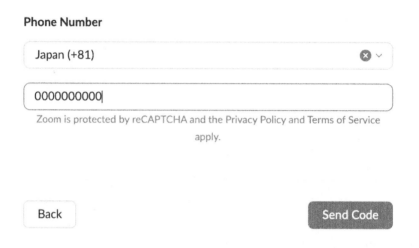

Phone Number

| Japan (+81) | ⊗ ⌄ |

| 0000000000| |

Zoom is protected by reCAPTCHA and the Privacy Policy and Terms of Service apply.

| Back | Send Code |

SMS authentication settings

The last thing Zoom will display are the recovery codes you can use in case you can't get back in to your account. Keep those in a VERY safe place. Choose either option, download or print, and click **Done**.

2.7 SHOULD I USE A PASSWORD MANAGER?

Absolutely yes. Yes... YES!

If you have not started using a password manager (software that securely stores and helps you remember passwords for all of your accounts), you are running your online life at quite a risk, and it's totally unnecessary. Heaven forbid you are still using the same password for more than one account. I stopped doing that around 1998.

You should always be using a password that is more complex than the minimum recommendations of the software. I started doing that around 2005.

If you are doing all that, you're going to need a password manager to hold all of those passwords for you. They're very convenient because even the free one that comes with a Mac both recommends strong passwords for new accounts and remembers them whenever you have to enter them. Microsoft Windows has a password manager as well, and you are not at loss for choices should you wish to get even better third-party commercial software for this purpose.

However, third-party password managers cost more money, and for most people's purposes, the one that came with your computer is fine. Just start using it.

2.8 HOW CAN I USE REMOTE CONTROL?

Before we begin, go to your Zoom website settings right now and find the switch for **Remote Control**, and if it is not yet turned OFF, go and turn it off right now.

Passing remote control to another user

Good. Now let me explain. Zoom since at least about late spring 2020 had a feature available that allowed a user to hand over control of their cursor and keyboard to another Zoom user during a meeting. In its first implementation, it was limited and a little inconsistent in behavior. I tried it a few times and didn't think much of it. I was really hoping it would work out because potentially it could be an amazing tool to help any students or friends who were having trouble doing something on Zoom. Unfortunately, I'm sure you can imagine the extreme potential it has for wrongdoing, especially for users who aren't even aware that it exists.

I recently revisited the Zoom remote control function and was surprised how much it has matured. It can give the remote controller control over potentially all of another user's computer if the controlled user is not careful. It would be a great service to your students and even peers to tell them that they too should disable remote control, and turn it on only when they need it.

Instructions below are separated into different headings, but if you are doing this for the first time, I recommend reading this entire section before you begin trying it yourself. Then actually do a test meeting with a friend or with your second device to see what it's like. In a pinch, it might be able to help you solve a student's technical problem much more quickly than explaining to them what to do with only your voice or your screen share.

When you're done with any remote control session, promptly go back to your account's website setting and turn off **Remote Control**, then restart Zoom on your computer to engage the settings.

HOW DO I START REMOTE CONTROL (RC)?

Remote control
During screen sharing, the person who is sharing can allow others to control the shared content

☑ Allow remote controlling user to share clipboard ☑

How to turn on Remote control access

First go to your Zoom account's website settings and turn on **Remote Control**. The next time you start up Zoom and engage screen sharing, you'll see the **Remote Control** button in the screen sharing toolbar. You can choose to automatically accept any requests for remote control, or you can look at the lower menu of eligible users and choose one from there.

The Remote Control option

WHAT DO I NEED TO DO TO ALLOW RC ON MY MAC?

The first time you try to allow Zoom's RC, your computer will ask you to adjust its **Accessibility Access** settings to allow Zoom to run your computer via commands from someone else's. This is an extra layer of security that Macs use to make sure that the person about to give up remote control is sure they really want to do it.

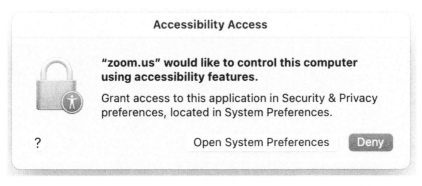

The Macintosh Accessibility Access panel

First, your Mac will tell you that Zoom is requesting access to your Mac's **Accessibility** controls. Click the left button, **Open System Preferences**. You'll then go to the System Preferences for **Security & Privacy**, and the **Accessibility** section will be highlighted on the left.

If the lock icon on the bottom left indicates closed, click it and enter your Mac's passcode to open it for editing. Scroll until you see the icon for zoom.us, and click the checkbox next to it, and it will turn blue. This gives Zoom the access it needs.

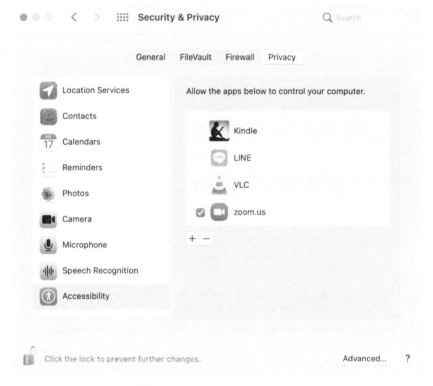

Accessibility options in Security & Privacy preferences

Before you leave **System Preferences**, click the lock icon again to secure your settings.

WHAT DO I NEED TO DO TO ALLOW RC ON MY PC?

This is where it gets a little scary. Above, you can see that when enabling Zoom remote control the first time on a Mac, you have to jump through a few hoops where your computer is giving you all kinds of warnings that what you are about to try might be a bad idea. Granted, a really skilled scammer can find ways to keep convincing you to continue with their instructions, which is why it's important to make it known that Zoom can do this.

A Windows PC, however, has no requirements to bypass security settings or warnings that Zoom remote control is a security risk. If a user's website settings are still on their default setting to allow remote control, RC can be engaged immediately on a PC, and remarkably on the Linux version of Zoom as well.

WHAT DO I NEED TO DO TO ALLOW RC ON MY MOBILE DEVICES?

Mobile devices like tablets and phones can act as remote controllers, but by the nature of their functionality and security settings, cannot hand over remote control to anyone else. This goes for any such device, Android or iOS.

PART 3

THE DIGITAL STAGE

When I found myself being asked for advice on remote teaching, there were few things I could draw on for reference. There were basically no instructors around me experienced in remote education that I could talk to even as my online presence grew. Instead, I came to the attention of others as someone who knew what they were doing with Zoom even as I was scrambling myself to figure out how I should answer the questions people were asking me.

With little that I could use as a base of knowledge, I found myself going back to what I learned in places as varied as the junior high school drama club. My teacher Ellen Matte taught us all about lighting, facing the audience, projecting your voice, and knowing how to be on stage. Luckily, at our junior high it was cool to be in the drama crowd and it was even cooler to be good at knowing how to hold an audience's attention.

I think more instructors, especially in the world of remote teaching, could do with a bit of the knowledge that Ms. Matte imparted to us. To some students, looking at their computer is not that far removed from looking at a TV or movie screen, and even if subconsciously, I think they might be judging their teachers by similar standards.

Of course it isn't necessary to learn iambic pentameter or anything, but it does help to consider yourself as being on stage. Making sure that we pay due attention to the points in this unit could help a lot of us who want to improve our remote teaching.

3.1 SHOULD AUDIO BE MY TOP PRIORITY?

Yes. If you want to start making improvements to your Zoom classroom, the first place you should be focusing your efforts is in your overall audio presence. When you're watching a video or a movie on the internet, what do you find more grating: bad audio or bad video? If you chose bad audio, you're not alone, as most people will agree that it's more of a reason to stop watching a video. I often come into Zoom calls in academic conferences where I can really hear the difference in audio quality between those who have invested time in making a good environment and those who haven't.

"Bad sound" in a Zoom class means that you hear lots of echoes and extraneous noise, and perhaps the speaker's voice is weak or too far away from the microphone. So first, while it might be inconvenient, try to find a workspace that is away from family noise or open windows. If you have a lot of flat walls with hard surfaces, try rearranging some shelves or pieces of furniture to break up the echoes. Hanging cloth over large areas of bare wall or closing the curtains can help, but be careful you don't make the room too dark. That just trades one problem for another. Experiment with where your workspace is located and see if adjusting its location can improve the sound environment.

In our plays, Ms. Matte watched over us as we learned how to deliver our lines well. One no-no was "stepping" on someone's lines—saying your next line before the other person has finished theirs. Zoom can only handle one audio stream at a time. Other sounds will get sent to the background and won't be heard; or worse, all of the audio can get garbled and it gets hard to figure out who even said what. Resist the urge to speak unless you clearly know that you can do so without stepping on anyone. If you have a habit of saying a lot of things like "Right!" and "Is that so!" while someone is speaking, that confuses the audio system if you're not muted. In a normal conversation, those utterances are considered part of cooperative acknowledgement and can be quite welcome to a speaker to tell them that what they're saying is being well received. In Zoom, however, they can be quite confusing. Either eliminate them or mute yourself so the microphone doesn't pick them up.

Avoid locations where the microphone is too exposed to the sound of your air conditioner or fan. One thing that makes built-in microphones suffer is when the computer starts to get hot and the computer's fans start working harder. Zoom has excellent default noise suppression, but if it has to really kick into overdrive to take out the fan noise, then your voice quality will be further compromised.

I talk more about audio in Part IV: The Equipment Issue.

3.2 HOW IMPORTANT IS MY VIDEO?

It's not at all important if your camera is off. But if you intend to show yourself to your students—and you should—this is obviously the next thing to consider for improving your "stage presence."

Let's begin with your camera placement. As I said before, there wasn't much that we should have expected out of teachers back in the spring of 2020 as everyone struggled to stay afloat with Emergency Remote Teaching (ERT). Forgiveness and compassion weren't just for our students, but for ourselves as well. But by now we should have seen enough online seminars and conferences and classes to know that some people just look better on their Zoom camera than others.

The first and easiest thing you can do is set your web camera square to your shoulders and *at just slightly higher than eye level.* With most desktop computers now having a built-in webcam, this shouldn't be too difficult, but too often I still see some who use a notebook (laptop) computer at an angle that makes the instructor look as if they are looking down at their audience. I have been in online seminars with people who used a tablet computer to attend, placed the tablet down flat on their desk, and had the camera pointing almost right up their nose—not a flattering angle.

Instead, if you are using a notebook, look for items you can put under the notebook to raise it up, like a stack of big books or a shoebox. This may make using the keyboard and trackpad a bit more awkward, but most instructors won't actually be typing much during their instruction sessions. If the need warrants, there are always wireless keyboards and pointing devices that you can add later.

3.3 WHAT MAKES A GOOD SHOT FRAME?

In February of 2021, a video went viral of a raucous parish council meeting in the British town of Handforth in Cheshire. (Several recordings of this can easily be found with a quick search on YouTube.)

Apart from the obvious bullying that was being heaped upon the hero of the incident, Jackie Weaver, one of the things that struck me was how all of the acrimony was coming from members poorly framed in their Zoom cameras. In contrast, Ms. Weaver and her allies knew how to present themselves on a webcam. On the other side, the disrespectful, angry men had their cameras not only pointing up in exactly the way I was telling you above *not* to do, they were not sitting square to their webcams, and one had his face so close to the camera you could practically feel his anxiety. Another began the meeting unaware that it had started and had his back to the audience.

Don't be like those guys. Be like Jackie Weaver.

Ms. Weaver had her camera at eye level. Her face was centered vertically but in the upper third horizontally. The top of her head was close to, but under the upper edge of the frame. Moreover, she had a nice head-and-shoulders composition that allowed her to look like a newscaster, and she didn't have her head so close to the camera that it appeared disembodied. If you want a confirmation that this makes a good professional-looking frame, take a close look when you watch the evening news tonight and you'll see all of these points outlined again right in front of you.

If there was one thing I would have adjusted about Ms. Weaver's camera frame, it would have been to have it set more square to her shoulders, down the center vertical line of her chest. She was probably using that angle because her camera was not built into the monitor she was looking at.

Aiming for this head-and-shoulders frame not only makes you look more professional, it keeps your face from becoming too imposing, and if you're big on gestures like I am, it makes not only your hands easier to see moving around in your camera, but also documents or items that you wish to show your audience.

A well-centered frame

One other caveat: if you have the luxury of having a multi-monitor setup, be careful that you don't do anything but glance for a few seconds at documents or other computer windows on the monitor that is not holding your webcam. Looking at documents on a

46

second monitor for extended periods makes you appear as if you are not looking at your audience. As a communication teacher, I tell my students that is faux pas #1.

PRO TIP: *To get better eye contact with the camera, place your zoom meeting window right under where your webcam is, not to the side or lower part of your monitor. When you share your screen, place the Zoom camera preview grid in that position.*

3.4 WHAT SHOULD I TAKE INTO CONSIDERATION WITH LIGHTING?

Roughly speaking, the more light you can cast on yourself during a Zoom meeting/class, the better. But just as there is obviously a point where there isn't enough light to make you look good, there's also a point where there's too much. Most people, however, fall into the former category.

One of the hardest things to get used to in our junior high plays was the stage lights, but after a few minutes of blinking clumsiness, we all eventually got accustomed to the lights and trained ourselves to accept them as part of what makes a theatrical play.

A good lighting setup for Zoom meetings will do the same thing. At first, you might feel a little put off, but in one minute or less, it will become easy to ignore. You can certainly go ahead without extra light on your image—many people do—but sometimes the difference in image improvement can be dramatic, especially if your webcam does not have the capability to work well in low light.

To add lighting to your Zoom setup, you don't have to acquire anything in terms of specialized equipment. I had an old articulating arm lamp that I bought at a certain Swedish furniture shop that could I put on my desk behind my iMac, about 3-4 cm to one side of the web camera position.

While considering the overhead room lights and the light coming in from windows, play around with the placement angle, paying attention to any shadows from your nose or glasses. If the light is too harsh, try jury-rigging or taping some sheets of paper in front of the lamp to moderate any unnecessary brightness. If you're buying the lamp and the bulb new, try to purchase a lamp color that is toward the "warmer" (yellow) side.

Speaking of glasses—many people have taken to purchasing ring lights, as ring lights can impart a nice, even light on a camera's subject. That's true, but be aware that if you wear glasses, the image of the ring light can often be clearly seen reflected on your lenses.

Ring lights also require that the camera be positioned in the center inside the ring light's circle, to get their best effect. Trying to do that with a built-in webcam is simply a wasted effort. You should be able to rig a smartphone camera to position itself inside a ring light to achieve the desired effect, but if you're not willing to make that effort, there's no particular reason to spend extra money on a ring light, even though they do impart a nicer, softer light than most other lamps.

One more thing about lighting: Watch out for lighting coming behind you, like from a bright window, and don't light yourself primarily from a sharp angle, as then you get too many shadows falling across your face. Especially avoid light that's originating from below the camera position, unless you want to look like you're about to tell horror stories around a campfire.

3.5 HOW CAN I USE VIRTUAL BACKGROUNDS MORE EFFECTIVELY?

You've probably already used virtual backgrounds (VBs) before, if you need to set up somewhere other than your usual space because of noisy construction next door or the kids using the dining room table for homework. So you know that it's not hard to work with VBs, but I do have a couple of hints when you use them.

First, make sure you have good lighting on your image. If you use a VB of a sunny beach, but your own image is dark, it makes for an odd mix. Avoid using movies as virtual backgrounds, as they will take up more bandwidth for everyone and more memory on your own computer to run them.

I don't use a green screen myself, as I'm lucky to have a set-up at home that has a nice, relatively quiet background. If you are going to use a green screen, though, make sure it doesn't have too many folds in it and that the screen itself is evenly illuminated, covers all of your background, and isn't fluttering from an electric fan or AC. Any kind of green cloth will do as long as it hangs evenly. I've seen pictures of people's setups where they jury-rigged green screens with laundry poles and carpenter's clamps, and all of them looked great. I've seen good results from screens that are designed to attach to the back of your chair. If you have money to burn, Elgato or other manufacturers make really nice compact folding green screens, but they can be expensive, starting at around US$150 or so.

3.6 WHAT ELSE CAN I DO WITH VIRTUAL BACKGROUNDS?

Many people use virtual backgrounds mostly to hide the breakfast dishes or whatever else behind you that nobody needs to see. I discovered though that they also make a handy place to put information that's useful for class—for example, a quote or a chemical formula that you'll be discussing that day. In the image on the next page I outlined the parameters of a writing assignment.

If you look at Zoom's own specifications for VB size, the maximum dimensions are 1920 x 1080 pixels. If you make an image to that size in an image editor, like Pixelmator for Mac or the GIMP for any platform, you can then export it as a file to your computer. If you intend to keep that custom VB around, make a folder inside the Zoom folder where the transcripts go because if the file moves from where Zoom was first told it was, you'll have to tell Zoom once again the file's location. You can achieve something similar with Sharing Slides as a background (see below), but if you only need to share one page of information, this could be a snappier alternative.

Writing Assignment:

write a paper on Shiina's article
about Abe's two-mask idea.

- handwritten
- 30 minutes writing time
- when finished, take a picture right away and show
me the picture by submitting it under Shiina's post on FB Happy!.
- retype on GOOGLE docs, and share it with me.

jdmcruz@gmail.com

Due Date for rewrite: Monday April 27, 10:00

(3)

GOLDFish**365 Happy!**

A slide as a virtual background

You'll need to sit on one side while you display it, but you don't need to keep the image up for the entire class. You could have one image just to show what that lesson's objectives are and show that for the first five minutes. Then another one that describes the homework could be up for the last five minutes.

Take a look at the next image and imagine that it's a VB movie. I used it to make a screencast of just the area where the students need to change their names in Zoom, so they can change it back to their real name as opposed to whatever goofy moniker they used for their buddy's Zoom party.

I started the video from the first step, in which they click on their name in the participants list and they could follow the cursor as it clicked and moved until the name change was complete. I put it into iMovie on my Mac and changed it into a smaller size (picture-in-a-picture) and put it off to the side. I still had to show them all the first time in class, but after that I only needed to remind them while the video played behind me.

A video used as a virtual background

VBs can be used quite creatively, so I was pretty excited to hear that around November 2020, Zoom improved VBs further by making it an option to use slideshows from PowerPoint or Keynote as VBs. The feature is actually still in Beta mode, but even with a couple of limitations, it works quite well. I talk about it in detail in the section on Advanced Screen Sharing.

PART 4

THE EQUIPMENT ISSUE

The equipment issue can be quite a rabbit hole if you're not careful. I know some people that, in a sincere desire to have better classes, focused a little too much on their hardware and spent way more money and time than they needed to, and in the end only made the same gains in their overall pedagogical quality as people who used much less.

Spending more on any of the recommendations in this section is not any guarantee of improvement in what matters most—becoming the best teacher you can be.

So here's a friendly reminder:

- Have you tried making the adjustments to your teaching environment that I talked about in Part III: The Digital Stage?
- Have you cleaned up your quizzes and materials presentations in your LMS?
- Have you done a few test recordings of your teaching in

Zoom and watched them so you can see yourself as your students see you?

- Can you improve what you noticed is your sometimes-weak voice or your tendency to talk to yourself as you do something on the computer while your students are watching you?
- Have you learned how to teach while you look not at your own image but at the web camera in your computer?

Those are all improvements you can make and should make to your digital presence even before, or at least alongside any new equipment additions. If, however, you've done your best to address those issues, take a look below at what else you can change.

4.1 HOW CAN I CHOOSE A GOOD MICROPHONE?

First, make sure you started by doing what you can to improve your audio environment as discussed in Part III: The Digital Stage. If you've made all the environmental adjustments that I recommended, you're probably wondering if the built-in microphone is good enough. Good question. That answer has qualifiers, but in general I would say it isn't good enough. Using the built-in mic is certainly convenient, and if you don't have the budget to get an external mic, then there's not much you can do but start saving up.

In terms of sound quality, the wired earphones you probably received with your smartphone actually have a pretty good mic. If you find yourself short of cash but wanting a better microphone, try using those. Record a Zoom session using the mic and listen to the sound quality with the headset and without. Then you can start to hear the differences that will help you decide what's best for your computer and meeting environment. The one caveat I make, and it has more to do with my aesthetic preferences than anything scientific, is that I don't like the way anyone really looks doing a video and speaking to the camera while wearing headphones.

If you've tried a preliminary test video over Zoom with your phone headset, and still think that you want something better than your computer's mic, see if any of your peers near you have similar computer setups and ask them for recommendations, and more importantly, see if you can borrow their mic for an experiment on your setup. If it sounds good to you, save yourself any more trouble and go with what you've already tried and will be satisfied with. A verified hands-on experience is worth more than a recommendation at a distance.

WHAT MICROPHONE BRANDS CAN YOU RECOMMEND?

Let's say you have no one to borrow equipment from. First, consider your budget. External computer audio can go from inexpensive desktop mics to full-on, recording-studio-quality systems. If you're a music teacher who already has some good microphones and other equipment, you should be able to adapt some of that over a USB mixer into your computer. Decent and simple DAC (Digital/Analog Converter) mixers are available starting at about US$150. Those will take any studio microphone and connect it via XLR cable to the mixer and then into your computer. If you understood the previous few sentences, I don't think I need to tell you any more, as you probably know more than I do about studio setups.

Sony and Audio-Technica have quite a few USB desktop mics with a stand that you can purchase for around US$30-$40. Those will do fine, but if you tend to tap your pencil or move around a lot of materials on your desk, a stand without a shock mount will take all those noises on your desk, and sometimes even the sounds of you typing, and send them straight into the microphone. Look for a microphone that has a shock mount included in the price.

I have a mid-level quality Audio-Technica microphone mounted on an articulating boom arm I connected to my iMac that I use for my podcast and important Zoom broadcasts or videos. Almost ten years ago, I got one of those Blue Yeti mics that many teachers ended up getting during 2020, as they heard (quite rightly) that the Yeti is a good, simple solution and provides great sound. It still works fine. It's a great mic, but a little bulky on my desk, especially as I use it with its shock mount. Yet in the end what I've come to use as my go-to mic when I'm teaching or presenting is my lavalier mic.

4.2 WHY DO YOU RECOMMEND A LAVALIER MICROPHONE?

A lavalier microphone is one of those really small microphones that you see pinned to a person's necktie or shirt during TV interviews. They can be so small and unobtrusive that they're practically invisible. In such applications they're usually wireless, but for most teachers sitting at their desks, a mic cable isn't a big deal, so there's no need to opt for that more expensive option.

I prefer lavalier (lav) mics for several reasons. They're small and thus don't provide anything more to distract bored students. They don't take up any space on your desk or block your view of your notes or your computer. A lav mic pinned to your clothing is unlikely to pick up as many noises like pens or books being moved on your desk as a conventional microphone not on a shock mount would. It's easier for you to move around at your desk without worrying that if you get too far from your stationary mic or even if you just turn your head, your voice will get too small.

My preferred lav mic is called the RODE SmartLav+. It's designed for smartphones, but comes with an adapter to work with conventional 3.5mm (1/8") microphone input terminals. It's a little pricey, at anywhere from US$70-90 depending on where you purchase it, but RODE is a good maker and the sound quality comes close to my best mics. You can connect it to your computer with any kind of USB to 3.5mm audio adapter. Those go for about US$10-15.

One particular advantage about the RODE Smartlav+ is that you can purchase a headset for it that converts it from a position close to your sternum to one just to the side of your mouth. Not immediately necessary while we are teaching from home, but in some schools, administrators are considering hybrid or hyflex classroom arrangements that might necessitate being able to speak simultaneously both to students in the classroom and those who are attending via Zoom.

My friend and neurodiversity expert Alexandra Burke pointed out that we should actually always be using microphones in our classes except for the smallest seminars, as without our knowing it, we might have students in class with hearing disabilities. Students sometimes go about their lives without having been diagnosed with such a problem, yet would receive great benefit nonetheless from having the teacher's voice amplified in the classroom even after the need for social distancing is over.

4.3 SHOULD I GET SPEAKERS OR HEADPHONES?

I personally recommend that you go with external speakers for your setup. As long as you have the desk space, a pair of powered speakers is not expensive. They start at about US$70 for a good pair. I much prefer them over headphones, which can get hot and uncomfortable in the summer, and if you get a headset marketed for video gaming, they tend to have very garish designs that I suspect might be distracting for students after a while. The gaming headsets also tend to have poor microphone quality, with user voices sounding over-amplified or "clipped."

A pair of external speakers makes all of your computer's sound output better, making movies and music more pleasurable.

If, however, you have a small apartment, you might not want to have the sound of your classroom on top of the sound of your teaching voice as an additional distraction for others in the next room. Then perhaps a pair of headphones might be in order. However, I'd still suggest staying away from the fire engine red headphones that make you look a bit like Princess Leia experimenting with her hair color.

4.4 WHAT IS THAT ECHO I SOMETIMES HEAR IN MEETINGS?

Sometimes you'll hear an odd echo of your own voice or other people's voices during a meeting. It's hard to tell who might be causing it because the echo can manifest itself in different ways. Sometimes the person with the faulty audio has an echo when they speak, but sometimes the faulty audio causes everyone else but the speaker in the meeting to hear an echo.

If it's a persistent echo, then you'll want to try to fix it. If you're the host and want to make yourself look like a Zoom guru, you can first figure out whose mic is at fault by selectively muting people. If the echo consistently goes away when a particular individual is muted, the problem is probably with that person's audio.

Once you know who it is, ask them to go to their app settings and look in the audio category. There in the section under **Music and Professional Audio**, there is a checkbox second from the bottom labeled **Echo cancellation**. Make sure they have that checked, and the echo should go away.

Music and Professional Audio

☑ Show in-meeting option to "Turn On Original Sound" from microphone ⑦

Enable these options when original sound is on

☐ High-fidelity music mode ⑦

☑ Echo cancellation ⑦

☐ Stereo audio ⑦

Echo cancellation

4.5 WHAT DOES THE "LEAVE COMPUTER AUDIO" MENU ITEM DO?

Leave Computer Audio pauses all your audio going into and coming out of the meeting. Beyond its obvious purpose of letting me pause audio even while I'm still watching what's on screen, I also use it when I want to enter the same meeting on another device.

If you take no special measures against it, two devices in close proximity in the same meeting will potentially create a feedback "howl" through all the meeting's participating devices. The easiest way to prevent that in a standard manner is before you join a meeting with the second device, make sure that you choose the **Leave Computer Audio** menu item on the device that's already in the meeting. This will keep the howl from happening.

Once both devices are in the meeting, you can then select which device will be your primary audio device for that meeting. Note: On mobile devices, the equivalent menu item is accessed by first tapping the **More** button, and in the menu that appears, choose **Disconnect Audio**.

4.6 HOW DO I FIX THAT CRACKLING SOUND?

I have several microphones connected to my Mac, all of them through USB. At random times, people will tell me in a meeting that whenever I say anything that they are hearing a strange crackling sound. It doesn't happen often, and I think it's associated with me using several different mics, as I've never heard this problem arise with anyone unless they have attached an external microphone.

If it comes up, click the up arrow icon next to your microphone button at the bottom left hand corner of the Zoom window. A pop-up menu will appear, and at the top section of the menu, you will find your microphone selection menu. Find your microphone choices and choose any microphone other the one you're currently using.

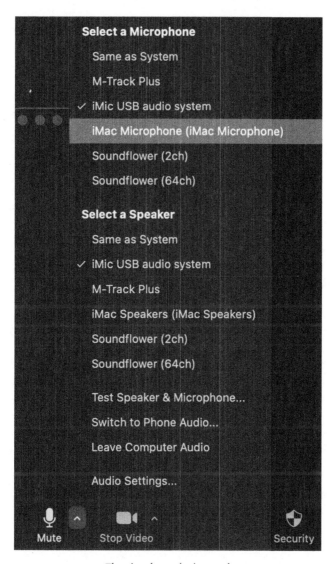

The microphone selection panel

If you only have one microphone, you should be able to choose the computer's built-in mic. That should immediately make the problem go away. Confirm that it did with your meeting participants. Then return to the mic selection menu and go back to your microphone of choice. The problem should be gone—at least until the next time it chooses to say hello.

4.7 WHY CAN'T MY STUDENTS HEAR ME PLAY THE GUITAR?

If you occasionally try to brighten up your classes with a few bars or a whole song in your classes, and find that the sound of your guitar or flute is broken up by the time it gets to the audience, that's Zoom's noise cancellation and echo suppression kicking in. You can control all of that in your audio settings.

However, if you want to toggle your settings easily between playing music and speaking without a lot fidgeting with controls, look at the **Audio** section in your application settings under **Music and Professional audio.**

The first checkbox is labeled **Show in-meeting option to "Turn On Original Sound" from microphone.** Checking that will give you a new button in the top-left of the meeting window next to the green shield.

Music and Professional Audio

☑ Show in-meeting option to "Turn On Original Sound" from microphone ⓘ

    Enable these options when original sound is on

    ☐ High-fidelity music mode ⓘ

    ☑ Echo cancellation ⓘ

    ☐ Stereo audio ⓘ

The "Turn On Original Sound" option

When **Original Sound** is being used, all of Zoom's systems for automatically controlling volume and noise to optimize voice interaction in meetings will be suppressed, so the audience will hear everything—from your harmonica to your air conditioner.

You can also choose a specific microphone to use with **Original Sound** by clicking on the down arrow to the right of the **Turn on Original Sound** button. After I tested it and found it works, I now leave the button up all the time, as I might find it handy one day, and it doesn't affect anything unless I purposely click it.

4.8 SHOULD I UPGRADE MY CAMERA?

Compared to your audio system, I think cameras are less important as a target for upgrades. You can do so much more to improve your digital stage by thinking about your microphone and speakers; your camera height, angle, and position; and lighting. Just improving your lighting can really improve your camera image, as many cameras don't do well in low light. Of course, none of that is as important as paying attention to adapting your teaching material and style to make a good class.

But let's say you do need a new camera; for example, if your built-in webcam has gone AWOL even though the rest of your computer is still OK. In that case, I would ask first if it might be time to buy a new computer. Then you will probably not only get a better camera but also a faster computer and maybe more disk space.

If you are hunting for a new computer, look for one that has an HD-quality camera. If you want even better than that, look for one that has a resolution of 1080px by 1920px or what is sometimes referred to as 2K resolution. Higher resolution cameras usually have better low light performance, which is important in darker rooms or evening classes.

Consider connecting your DSLR or mirrorless camera to your computer over USB. If your still camera can output its camera image over HDMI, you can get an adapter to convert the signal to USB, and Zoom will be able to see the camera as an option. A longer HDMI cable can get the camera to a remote location for special applications.

You will almost always get a nicer video image with a DSLR than with a built-in webcam. Makers like Nikon and Canon make software downloadable to your computer that lets Zoom connect to them directly via USB. Connecting the camera will take a few minutes, however, and some fiddling with software, so check with your camera maker's website or the shop where you bought the camera for information specific to your model.

You'll need some way to keep the camera in position with a tripod or other equipment. Some still cameras lose their autofocus ability when being used for video; be careful and as always, do lots of testing using Zoom recordings to confirm your setup.

4.9 DO MULTIPLE MONITORS MAKE ZOOM EASIER?

Having multiple monitors on your desk makes almost any computer work easier. Having multiple monitors is like getting a bigger house. You just have more room for your furniture and stuff, and everything can be more easily and strategically placed. The problem is that in the case of remote teaching, your students are watching you as you move your attention and your eyes from one monitor to another.

I know some people who have installed up to four monitors on their desks just for their remote teaching. The visual effect for the students is that they see their teacher moving their eyes all over the place: up and down, left and right.

Worse, some teachers have their web cameras mounted on top of the central monitor but have placed class lists or important information on a monitor to the side, so they're not looking into the camera and instead are showing their profile a good amount of the time. Personally I think this leaves the students with an impression that the teacher is less attentive to them, whether they know the teacher is using multiple monitors or not.

So while multiple monitors are certainly something I wouldn't mind for my own workspace at home, I would suggest that when you are teaching, keep all your necessary materials on one monitor to not exacerbate the problem of psychological distance between you and your students.

4.10 WOULD A SECOND COMPUTER BE USEFUL?

I'm not at all recommending that you go out and buy a second computer (for example, a notebook to sit beside your desktop).

However, not only can a second computer be a lifesaver in case your main one develops a problem that keeps it offline, but having another computer or a tablet beside you makes it easier to see class lists or lesson plans, notwithstanding my point in the previous section about making sure you keep your eyes focused on where the web camera is mounted.

Some of my friends have made a habit of having two devices in all their Zoom classes. One is their main computer, and the other is their tablet or even their phone.

The second device serves as a co-host through the meeting in case of something like a weak internet connection dropping the signal to the main computer, or perhaps to serve as a way to quickly check on breakout room activity while keeping your main computer in the main meeting room.

Just make sure that if you want your second device to be a desktop or notebook computer, that it is logged in from a second Zoom account, using a different email address. Zoom will not allow two devices of the same type to use the same account in the same meeting. A computer, a tablet, and a phone are considered different devices, however, and can join the same meeting at the same time using the same Zoom account.

4.11 WHAT OTHER TOYS MIGHT I CONSIDER?

If there's one thing I'd suggest to my peers to spend your research budget or hard-earned savings on, it's a large backup disk from a good maker. Do not skimp here. Do not buy the cheapest one you can find. If you want a small portable disk for carrying around, that's fine if you have the extra budget for it, but I'm talking about a good solid 4 or 8 terabyte (or better) hard disk with good specs. That can cost you around US$400, and that might sound expensive, but only if you think the grief and stress of losing your data in the middle of a semester is worth less than that.

If you have a Macintosh, set up the disk and search Apple's support pages on how to start and automate your backups with **Time Machine**.

On a Windows PC, the built-in software is called **File History** and **Backup and Restore**.

Do it now. Buy the disk and get a good reliable backup regimen going.

PART 5

ADDING TO YOUR ZOOM CLASSROOM SKILLS

I learned about Zoom in the same way I learned about Macs. I pushed a lot of buttons, I made a lot of mistakes, I read a lot of books, and I talked to a lot of friends.

Remember that the important thing to add to your online teaching expertise isn't about mastering Zoom or yet another piece of hardware. It's about learning how to teach better using all these new tools, and that often isn't written down in a book, because teachers and teaching styles are so wonderfully varied.

Teaching is the priority; Zoom is just a tool.

5.1 WHY DON'T MY STUDENTS TURN ON THEIR CAMERAS?

I often hear from my university peers in Japan that this is one issue they wish they could "fix" right away. Many will talk of how they spent most of their first few online classes talking to a black void of unresponsive Zoom avatars, all the while thinking about the appropriateness of changing their own profile pic to Munch's "The Scream."

Some schools in some countries reinforce this by actually preventing teachers from mentioning anything about turning cameras on, or actively telling students that having cameras on in synchronous sessions is entirely optional.

Conversely, some schools have opposite rules, where students are told they must have their cameras on at all times or they will not be counted for attendance.

I agree with my peers who say they have a hard time being motivated to teach a group of students who do not have their cameras on. Even during academic presentations, I much prefer speaking to an audience with their cameras on (and microphones off).

On the other hand, there are so many reasons students might not want to turn on their cameras, ranging from the easily understandable (*I have bandwidth issues*; *I have to nurse my newborn*) to less understandable (*I don't want to*; *You can't make me*). Students with slower computers or internet connections can experience issues with lag time, which can occur in a large class with everyone using gallery view.

I have to admit that when I first started to think about this issue, I wasn't experienced enough to consider more nuanced situations that involve confidentiality and privacy, and even issues of potential bullying and harassment around student's profile pics and stolen screenshots. Students might not want to reveal that they are attending class every week from a car parked outside a coffee shop. "I'm shy" could be a way of saying, "My anxiety is triggered every time I see my face on camera." Students who have spent their classroom lives learning how to cope with their neurodiversity issues, or how to hide their poverty from their friends well enough to make it through a normal classroom, are scrambling to know what to do in the virtual classroom. Sounds familiar, right?

I honestly can't say how I would cope with class upon class of students who don't turn on their cameras. If it happened, however, I would try to find a way to use my compassion for my students to try to understand their situation. In the case of a school that demands that students not even be approached to turn on their cameras, I understand how tough that might be to cope with, but I would imagine myself in one of my personal fantasies: standing on stage at TED, giving my long-awaited talk on my stellar teaching methods. (It's a fantasy. Stop laughing!) The audience is invisible in the darkened auditorium, but I know they are sitting there, nodding in agreement.

I also very often make prerecorded videos for my Moodle courses, and there I manage to keep up my stage presence without too much trouble. I don't think it would be impossible to use that psychological trick to help.

5.2 HOW CAN I ENCOURAGE STUDENTS TO TURN ON THEIR CAMERAS?

If it doesn't go against your school's rules, I suggest this method: At the start of the first few classes, ask your students to do a mic and camera check with you. Tell them you only need to check to make sure the hardware is working, as it will be important for subsequent breakout rooms or presentations or such later on that class (which of course is true).

Ask them to turn on their cameras and mics, and as you see their cam come on, call out their names with a greeting like "Good morning, Ms. Crittenden" or "Hello, Jennie" and require that they reply. If they don't reply, don't let it slip, as this is supposed to be a mic hardware check. Doing this might actually reveal a problem with their mic that would be best remedied before the class really gets underway. If you wish, you could extend the conversation with a couple of extra lines like, "Hey, did you find a house you like yet?" "How's the new car?" Mix the questions up; maybe sometimes asking interesting trivia questions: "What was Harrison Ford's job before he became an actor? What do you mean, 'Who's Harrison Ford?'" Or maybe have students prepare questions for you.

I found that in all of my synchronous classes, after I set this as a standard way for me to bring the students into my class, the act of seeing all their classmates turning on their cameras made it easier for students to overcome their own shyness to show themselves in the room.

DOES USING GALLERY VIEW HELP?

When I hear of teachers having trouble getting students to turn on their cameras, I wonder two things: first, have they actually taken the time to show students how to turn on gallery view in Zoom (top right-hand corner of the meeting window >> "View" button)? If I were a student and I never knew I had an option to view anything else but the teacher's big face in the Zoom window, I might be tempted to stop showing my camera too.

Also, this returns somewhat to my point about the digital stage. While most of us are comfortable and know how to project our best selves in front of live students, I wonder how many teachers who experience only a lukewarm response from students about turning cameras on remember to project a warm welcoming image. Have they perhaps fallen victim to a vicious cycle where they are disappointed by their audience reacting with blank video avatars, and thus start to reveal it in their faces and mannerisms? This then makes more students feel even more distant from the class and more prone to turn off their cameras, and the cycle spools into a tighter spin.

See this article from the *Washington Post* about one teacher's struggle to feel comfortable in classes with many cameras turned off.
https://wapo.st/30Kd5Dy

I make sure my students know that if there is a reason for them to turn off their cameras, such as bandwidth concerns or whatever worries they might have about showing themselves online, they only have to approach me and I will give them leave to turn off their cameras, or find some other way for them to feel more comfortable in my class.

I also try to take note of which students seem to be having trouble coming in and out of breakout rooms quickly, which is a symptom of a weak or unreliable internet connection. Helping students like that during class can raise your legitimacy with the class as someone who not only understands their problems but can help solve them.

5.3 HOW CAN I USE THE REACTIONS AT THE BOTTOM OF THE TOOLBAR?

Near the right-hand side of the meeting toolbar is a button labeled **Reactions**. It reveals a set of basic non-verbal reactions that a user can give during a meeting. Take a look at the screenshot. You've probably already used the thumbs up button before, to indicate that you're OK with what was said previously, or some of the other emoticons that you can see in the top row.

The Reactions toolbar

If you click any of those emoticons, they will show up in the top left-hand corner of your camera for ten seconds. If you click the **Raise Hand** button below them, however, your hand will stay up indefinitely until you click the **Lower Hand** button hand that has taken its place. Your hand might also be lowered by the meeting host if you forget to do so after asking your question or making your comment. In previous versions of Zoom, the **Raise Hand** button was in a slightly more inconvenient place at the bottom of the participants list.

That was also where Zoom kept another set of buttons that were activated only if you went to the website settings under **In Meeting (Basic) >> Non-verbal feedback**, which then gives an enhanced set of buttons that you can see in the next screenshot. Here you can now not only raise your hand, but between the emoticons and the raise hand button, there is now also a green check mark (√) and a red X. You can use these two, for example, to take rudimentary polls. The other buttons can indicate that you want the speaker or proceedings to either speed up or slow down.

Enhanced reactions

The middle row of enhanced reactions stays close to the left edge of the screen, and like the **Raise Hand** button, they stay up indefinitely until you click them again. If you click an emoticon and an enhanced reaction, they will both display next to each other on the top left-hand corner of the screen. Raised hands and enhanced reactions will also appear in the participants list. It's easier there to do response counts.

As an aside, those **Speed up** and **Slow down** buttons... I can't imagine how someone could use those buttons in a normal situation and not come off as a bit rude. That's not to say a positive use couldn't exist; it's just not something I have ever come across. Anyway, I suggest you use them with discretion.

5.4 HOW CAN I MAKE GOOD USE OF THE RAISE HAND BUTTON?

I use the **Raise Hand** button less in my EFL classes in Japan than I do when I am attending or running events for professional development or academic conferences. The culture of education in Japan doesn't much encourage university students to ask a lot of questions, I'm afraid.

I am often the room host in those latter situations, and the meetings are usually attended by 15 or more participants. In a meeting with such numbers, it is helpful to make sure that participants know how to indicate that they want to ask a question or make a remark by raising their hand using the button. Room hosts can see who has raised their hands either by looking for them in gallery view among the cameras visible in the meeting room or revealing the participants list where they appear to the right of the participant's name.

I find that in a meeting where many people are asking questions, the view of raised hands from the participants is more useful, as that shows in descending order the person who has had their hand up the longest, thus telling you who to call on next.

In the meeting room, the array of cameras will also change order, but the person who has had their hand up the longest will appear upper leftmost, and other raised hands will slide to the right of the newest. I find this ordering (newest on the upper left) to be less intuitive, but that is a personal preference.

As a room host for events, I find that most (not all) professional presenters prefer to take questions at set points within or at the completion of their presentation. Then when we arrive at one of those points, I coordinate with the presenter to tell them who has raised their hand to indicate a question waiting in the wings.

Once a person has spoken, they can lower their hand on their own (see above) or if they forget, you can lower it for them either by hovering your cursor over their name in the participants list or their video avatar in the meeting room, whereupon the **Lower Hand** button will appear.

In classes with students who are not very familiar with Zoom, it's a good idea to go over how to use the raise/lower hand buttons and any other features you think they will need, such as doing screen recordings or using breakout rooms, before you get too far into your class content.

5.5 HOW CAN MY STUDENTS SEE MORE OF EACH OTHER WHILE I'M SHARING?

If you're like me and think the students feel better about being in your online class if they can feel closer to their peers, you've probably wondered how to let them see more than just your screen and your lone picture while you are sharing a screen. You may have even had a student mention that to you directly. I know the whole idea of getting students to turn on their cameras is often discussed among us teachers, so if we feel more relieved seeing everyone's faces, I'm sure many students would too.

To let them see more of each others' reactions to a video or smiles and laughter at something humorous, first make sure that they know how to engage gallery view. Don't assume that your students know how to do this already. Then, tell them that during a screen share, they can see more cameras and in bigger sizes if they engage **Side-by-side mode** on their desktop or notebook computer. (See Part VIII for more on screen sharing.)

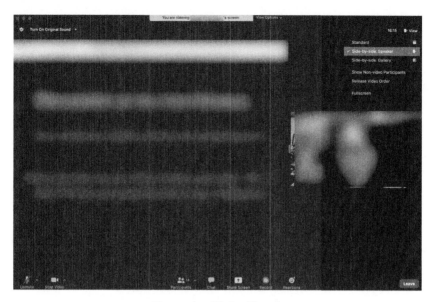

How to select Side-by-side mode

First show them where the setting is for side-by-side in the their application settings.

App settings>> Screen sharing>> Side-by-side mode

(fourth setting from the top)

Then show them how to find the **View** menu in the top right corner of their meeting window. There are two choices there during a screen share for side-by-side mode: S-by-S Speaker, and S-by-S Gallery. In either mode there is a pair of small white lines lying centrally between the shared image and the viewable participant cameras.

In S-by-S Speaker mode, dragging the two lines with your cursor will change the ratio of the speaker's camera view with the shared material. In S-by-S Gallery view, the cursor dragging will control both the size and the number of cameras viewable.

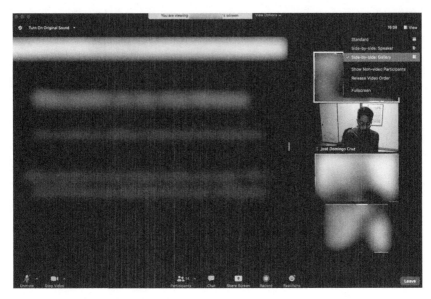

Side-by-side Gallery view

If you want to see more students, remember that in the video panel of participants, during your share you can click the button that looks like four cubes stacked together, and you can see the gallery view. This you can also resize and move around your own screen. You'll also have pagination arrows at the ends of the gallery view strip. Use them to run through all the cameras.

5.6 HOW DO I MAKE THE MEETING TOOLBAR STAY VISIBLE?

When you first enter a Zoom room, the first thing that strikes you is the number of buttons that appear in the meeting window. There are plenty enough when you are attending a meeting, but as teachers we get the full array of buttons that we can use as hosts.

You might also notice that after about five seconds, the controls will disappear until the next time you move your cursor. Zoom has this as the default setting so that you can mostly concentrate on the meeting, but as a teacher in a class, I find having the meeting controls (the **In-meeting Toolbar**) moving in and out of view every time I touch my trackpad slightly disorienting. By keeping the toolbar always in view, I have more information that I can use.

Always show meeting control toolbar

Always show meeting controls during a meeting ⓥ

Show Zoom windows during screen share ⓥ

To keep it on at all times, first turn the feature on in your account's website settings, **Always show meeting control toolbar.** While you're there, you might want to consider turning on the setting beneath it, **Show Zoom windows during screen share.** For this second setting to work, however, your computer must have the CPU and graphics power to handle it during a desktop screen share.

Go to your **Application** settings and under **General**, look for the checkbox (currently third from the top: **Always show meeting controls**) and make sure it is checked.

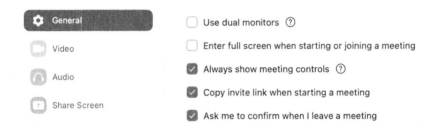

You can also manage the meeting toolbar by using command-], which will toggle the checkbox. Zoom also keeps a control for the in-meeting toolbar in the website settings, but as of version 5.5.5, the priority of control seems to lie with the application.

5.7 IS THERE ANYTHING I SHOULD NOTE ABOUT THE "MUTE" OR "STOP VIDEO" BUTTONS?

You probably already know enough that those buttons do exactly what they say. What many people don't know is that the up arrow button next to each one lets you get to frequently used setting controls related to meeting audio and video.

First note that either up arrow reveals, at the bottom of its respective popup menu, a way to easily get to the application settings for that part of Zoom. This means that via either menu item, you can easily get to any part of the application settings, such as **Recordings,** or quickly review the keyboard shortcuts for certain items or change your virtual background. It's also one method for quickly getting to the Zoom.us website.

For example, use **Audio Settings** to call up the application settings window, and then click the section **General**. At the bottom of that section, just under where you can choose reaction skin tones, is the blue **View More Settings** button. That will take you to your account's settings on the website.

5.8 WHAT CAN I DO FOR A CLASS WITH STUDENTS WHO ARE INTERRUPTING EACH OTHER?

You might already know that you can mute all students in a Zoom class with a menu item under the **Meeting** menu in Zoom. Like most people, though, in your hurry to get everybody to shut up, you might have overlooked a checkbox right under the blue **Mute All** button labeled **Allow participants to unmute themselves**. If you uncheck that, it'll prevent your noisy class from unmuting themselves until you allow them with the **Ask All to Unmute** menu item, or by selecting them individually from the participants menu.

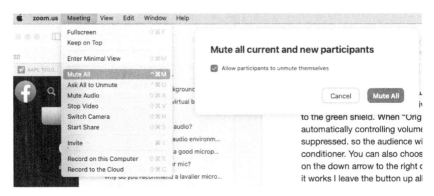

How to mute all students at once

Believe it or not, even though many of us have a hard time getting our students to speak up in remote synchronous classes, some teachers have the opposite problem. Apparently, it can be horrible. Life doesn't seem so bad on this side of the fence now.

If you want a bit more information about audio concerns, be sure to read Part III: The Digital Stage, and the section on Audio preferences in Part VII: Your Zoom Application Settings.

5.9 HOW CAN ZOOM PROVIDE SOCIAL OUTLETS FOR STUDENTS?

One of the challenges that instructors are faced with is looking after not only our students' educational needs, but to some degree their mental health as well.

During the pandemic, many university or K-12 students who were forced to stay home and take remote classes found the experience psychologically draining, as they were not allowed to do much of anything social with their friends; or in the case of students starting a new school, couldn't even make any friends. The need for such attention to mental health will abate as the pandemic recedes, but in the case of fully remote courses for rural areas or graduate school programs, it isn't a concern that should be readily dismissed, especially when there are some easy ways to help alleviate it.

Many students taking remote classes said it was difficult to deal with the isolation of attending school entirely on their computers, sometimes alone at home. Let's face it: remote education for a 15-year-old seems like school with all of the fun stuff (clubs, sports, friends) taken out, and all the bad stuff (homework, assignments) made worse by the lack of human presence. Sometimes it was compounded by the fumbling attempts of some institutions that insisted on making no changes in the curriculum, or worse, increased the amount of homework.

In this environment, I think it helps our students to hear a few kind words from us as teachers to tell them that we empathize, that we feel the strain of the situation too.

In some of my classes, maybe once or twice a semester, I would use the remaining 10 or 15 minutes of a class for students to use breakout rooms just to hang out with each other and talk about anything else completely outside of my curriculum. I was told by some students that it was a welcome chance to talk to some of their peers, as they were first-year students and hadn't even set foot on campus. Zoom was new to them, and they were glad to have someone organize a chance to chat with others. Before Zoom had self-select breakout rooms, I would just send them into random groups for five minutes at a time and let them talk to each other without me hovering over them. Other teachers I know handed over host control to a volunteer and let them have at it.

Schools should also consider that Zoom can be used as a virtual meeting place for at least some activities, such as chess clubs or book clubs. Students, when given the opportunity, will quickly adapt to what they can do in these virtual spaces without much in the way of administrative or parental oversight. The potential for problems in a virtual space are about as much as they are in a physical space, and if we can let the students self-govern them-selves there, I see no reason we can't trust them in the brave new world as well.

5.10 HOW SHOULD I BEST APPROACH MY ZOOM PROBLEMS?

My editor Dorothy Zemach would probably answer, "Call José." Seeing as how most of you don't have my phone number, though, let me give you a few approaches that will help you with handling not just Zoom problems but other tech-oriented issues as well.

So you have an annoying problem. First, take a deep breath. Then try to think analytically. What were you doing just before the problem appeared? Have you added new hardware or software recently? Are you trying a different feature of Zoom that you've never used before? If something unpredicted occurs in such situations, try to replicate the issue. Go over your steps and see if you went wrong somewhere, forgot to check a box, pushed the wrong button, etc.

What is the nature of the problem? Is it audio? Is it that your slides won't show? Either of those two examples could be connected to issues that exist outside of Zoom, so think about what or how you've done that could be affecting the issue.

When you're trying something new, leave mental breadcrumbs for yourself so that you know and can remember more easily how you arrived at whatever dialog box you are looking at or whatever webpage you seem to have landed on. If a dialog box appears for the first time, don't just push the default button without actually looking at the choices in front of you and thinking about all of the choices you have. There's no shame in taking notes, just like there's nothing wrong with buying instruction books. Remember that a lot of problems can be solved by just restarting the computer, or in this case, just restarting Zoom.

The internet houses most of the world's knowledge, and search engines now can actually take natural language queries and do quite well with them. Instead of having to think about what keywords will best return results like, "Zoom / meeting / full screen / no", you can write a normal question in the search engine's entry field like, "How do I keep Zoom from going full screen when I enter a meeting?"

Just like you sought the support of this book, seek cooperative online support groups. Lots of other people know things you don't. And you will find that you have ideas and suggestions that can help them too.

PART 6

YOUR ZOOM WEBSITE SETTINGS

When I refer to your website settings, I mean the options you can control when you login to your account on zoom.us. You'll see the sections tab vertically on the left, starting with **Profile**. Depending on which section you've chosen, you'll see another set of tabs arranged horizontally along the top. Clicking on one of the sections on the left will turn it blue, and you'll see the tabs for its subsections appear along the top.

If you have modified anything from Zoom's recommended **Settings** default, a notification will appear on the right, labeled **Modified**. To the right of that is a button to reset to default. This comes in handy if you need to be reminded about what you may have changed in the past. It's easy to get lost and confused when looking at all of these settings. Many teachers are quite technologically adept and others are not so, but almost all the peers that I have talked with consider Zoom to have an almost overwhelming amount of customization available.

Luckily, you don't have to know about all of these options, and what I want to do here is to give you a way to start looking at them so that you can more easily understand and manage them. Therefore, I'm not going to talk about *all* the items in the **Account Website** settings. Instead I'll skip over areas that already receive attention elsewhere in this book or may not be important to teachers, and move on to the next feature that deserves attention. Occasionally, though, give all these settings a look, because when Zoom introduces new features, they're often reflected with a new arrangement for the buttons in this area.

6.1 CUSTOMIZE WAITING ROOMS

A waiting room (WR) primarily serves a security function by allowing hosts a chance to see who is about to enter the room. It is Zoom's primary recommended measure against intruders. It can also serve as temporary holding facility for anyone you might want to put in it. It protects your meeting from intruders and problems, so much so that Zoom has WR as one of the three security features from which you must choose at least one to meet minimum security standards.

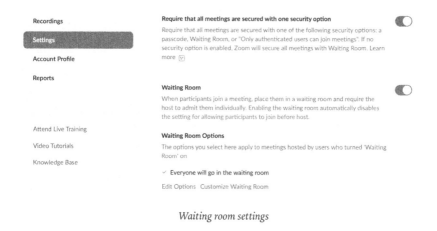

Waiting room settings

I noted early on that a WR can have its appearance and content customized somewhat. Last year, I used it to give my students a bit of a greeting before they entered. This year I'm using it to present interesting quotes, puzzles that they can answer for points, and messages they can read before entering the room.

To customize your room, you'll need to have a paid account. Go to your account website settings; near the top of your **Settings** is **Security**, where you'll find the **Waiting Room Options**. Make sure the actual WR is activated and then click the blue button for **Customize Waiting Room**.

There are four things in the subsequent customization dialogue box that you can edit. Three of them you can immediately edit by just clicking on the editing pencil next to them. The title header for your WR is at the very top and has a limit of 64 characters. Below that is where you can change your WR logo. The requirements for editing this graphic are outlined at the bottom of the dialogue box. The detail text is at the bottom and has a limit of 400 words. The fourth item is on the right with square brackets on either side and labeled **Your Meeting Topic**, and if like me, you're slow or under-caffeinated, you might spend a few minutes trying to figure out how to edit that particular item. Or if you're quicker on the draw, you'll realize that is where the title of the meeting goes. You can edit that every time you make a new meeting. The default is [**Your Name**]'s **Zoom Meeting**.

Welcome to Mr. Cruz's class. You will be let in soon.

José Domingo Cruz's Zoom Meeting

When you enter make sure your name is written in roman letters. If not please change it. Do a Microphone and camera check with Mr. Cruz. Make sure that he can hear and see you, then you can mute your microphone again. Make sure you have checked our Moodle for today's assignments.

The waiting room screen (a student's view)

PRO TIP: You can customize the WR image to display your logo, a graphic that is part of a brain teaser, or even a QR code that the students can use to go to a separate site.

From the 5.6.4 version of Zoom on, next to the button for customizing the WR appearance is a button labeled **Edit Options**, where you can fine-tune your WR settings. If you want to have a balance between letting students in speedily and ensuring security against intruders, some of these options might help you. Me, I'm going to stick with using WRs for everyone, and changing the content of the WR occasionally.

Customize your waiting room here

One interesting option that was added is at the bottom for moving participants to the WR if the host loses the connection. If you have a weak or unstable connection during class, this might be a good way to keep your students in the classroom while you reconnect and get back into your class through your account. Be sure to tell students that might happen, so that if it does, they don't get too confused and know that they should stay in the WR until you return.

6.2 WHAT MEETING ROOM SETTINGS DO YOU RECOMMEND?

Of course, these are a matter of personal preference, but I'll walk you through the reasons I made the decisions I did for some of these settings.

AUDIO TYPE

If you don't think you'll need to have students come into your classroom via voice call, you may as well set this option to **Computer Audio**.

ALLOW PARTICIPANTS TO JOIN BEFORE HOST

I teach mostly 1st and 2nd year university students. In Japan during the pandemic, many institutions that weren't familiar with remote instruction were sensitive to the potential problem of harassment and created rules to address these issues, but which also affected how teachers ran their classes. I do understand the root of their concern, and therefore I look for places where I can limit the opportunity for such problems to even arise.

One thing I did was turn off the option for students to join before me. I want to be there when they are assembled, especially for the first few classes when I'm still trying to gauge the psychology and makeup of each group.

UPCOMING MEETING REMINDER

I turn this off, as I have my calendar software send me notifications when my classes are about to start. Whatever you do, though, note that when dealing with international events that you calculate carefully to compensate for time zones.

ALWAYS SHOW MEETING CONTROL TOOLBAR

I find it useful to have this and the option below, **Show Zoom windows during screen share**, turned on during meetings. I find I can orient my eyes and hands to what button I want to push more quickly if Zoom doesn't hide them from me.

SHOW ZOOM WINDOWS DURING SCREEN SHARE

Along with the option above, **Always show meeting control toolbar**, I like to have this turned on. I address it further in the section on screen sharing.

ALLOW LIVESTREAMING OF MEETINGS

I find this a fabulous feature for teachers that combine Zoom with social media sites such as Facebook or YouTube.

Facebook private groups, when set as a "Social Learning" group and used judiciously, can work as a quasi-LMS for teachers who have no access to a real LMS of their own. I've used livestreaming to send a complete recording of everything that was on my Zoom immediately to Facebook. As soon as the Zoom session is over, Facebook archives the livestream as a recording for you in the Facebook group. YouTube handles your livestream the same way, and it can also be set to restrict access to only certain people.

6.3 HOW CAN I GET ALL THOSE PHONE NUMBERS TO STOP APPEARING IN MY INVITES?

Yeah, I hate those too. I'm sure they're useful for meetings that have people dialing in from all over the world, like major international press conferences. But if you're like me, you probably don't do a lot of those major international press conferences, so you'll be relieved to know there's a way to get rid of them.

Go to your Website settings. The tab you want is for **Telephone**, and the switch is at the top of that section: **Show international numbers link on the invitation email**.

6.4 HOW DO I MANAGE MEETING FUNCTIONS?

The **Meetings** tab on the left-hand side is just below the Profile section when you login to your account. Here you can find the list of all your meetings and perform management tasks on them.

WHY CAN'T I EDIT CERTAIN MEETING FUNCTIONS?

If you put your cursor over the title of any meeting in your meeting list, you'll see it indicated, and buttons to the right appear for editing and deletion. It may seem obvious that if you want to edit anything about a meeting, you click the **Edit** button, but there you will only find *most* of the details editable, not all of them. Most notably, if you want to enable certain features for the very first time, it's quite possible that first you have to go to the website settings to turn on that feature in your account; for example, polling or language interpretation.

Moreover, in the case of those two features, and perhaps others in the future, clicking the **Edit** button on a meeting will not take you to where you can edit the details. Instead you have to click on the title of the meeting in the list, and there you will find other buttons for editing **Polls** and **Interpretation** assignments near the bottom of the page. Meeting details are also where you can turn any meeting into a **Template**.

6.5 HOW DO I USE TEMPLATES?

Templates are worth the little bit of extra effort especially at the start of a school year or term when you have a lot of classes you want to put into a calendar, or that share similar settings. It doesn't take more than a minute to set a weekly recurrence of 16 classes, but it does get a little tedious if you have to do 12 of them at one school and 3 others for another school; and you have to do this twice a year for every semester.

Start creating a meeting the normal way. On the **Meetings** list page near the top right is a button labeled **Schedule a Meeting**. There as always, you can enter all of the meeting details you wish. Enter details like recurrences and security settings that you know you will need for other classes that will use this as a template, and then name the meeting clearly. Save it, and the page will refresh. Now you'll see the saved version of the meeting, and you at the bottom will appear the button to save it as a template.

Before you make it a template, though, double-check your settings and think about any poll questions you might want to include in all occurrences of meetings built from this template. When a template is made, the poll questions are also included, but they have to be made after the initial meeting is created. You can, however, add Polls to a template even after the template has been saved. In the dialogue box that appears when you click to save the template, make sure you check the box for **Save the recurrence** if that's what you want.

Once you save as a template, a version of this meeting will now be included in the **Template** list. If you edit the original meeting anytime after, you will have to resave it as a new version of the template if you want to include the new changes. You can't actually edit a template after you make it except to add polls.

After the template is made, it will appear in the **Template** list. Choose the template you want to use, and choose, not too surprisingly, **Use this Template**. From there the window will refresh with all the details from the template filled in but capable of being edited. If you click the **Save** button, it will save it as a new meeting.

PART 7

YOUR ZOOM APPLICATION SETTINGS

When I talk about application (app) settings, I mean the settings that can be adjusted within the Zoom software that you downloaded and installed on your computer. These app settings are affected by what you have set in your website settings. So for example, if you set your Security settings on the website to require that students be logged in to enter a new meeting that you are creating, that will be the default.

Yet in that case and in others, the app settings can override those website settings, so knowing what setting is where is rather important in learning how to more thoroughly master Zoom.

Most of them are fairly easy to understand, as their button labels are fairly self-explanatory. What makes them hard to use is that there are so many they can be overwhelming, and it's easy to lose the button you're looking for in the panel. I've therefore limited the discussion in this part to the buttons and checkboxes that I feel are important or of particular interest.

7.1 HOW DO I ACCESS MY APP SETTINGS?

There are actually a number of ways to access them; they differ according to your computer platform and whether or not you're in a meeting. While in a meeting, many people like to get to their app settings panel by clicking on the up arrow right next to the microphone button in the left corner of the meeting toolbar and clicking the menu item for **Audio Settings** at the bottom of the menu. That will take you to the **Audio** panel in the **App Settings** and from there, you can go anywhere else you wish.

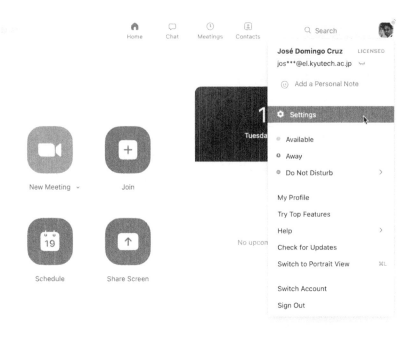

Navigating to settings via the Account menu

If you're not in a meeting, there are other ways to access settings, such as via the **Account** menu in the Zoom window. Click your profile picture in the top right corner of the Zoom window, and it will be the second item from the top. I recommend that you learn the keyboard shortcut for this: "Command-comma" for a Mac or "Control-comma" for a PC. Nothing is faster than the keyboard shortcut, and it works in all circumstances, in meeting or out, as long as Zoom is the frontmost application on your desktop.

---

*PRO TIP: A quick way to get to the website settings page is to call up the app settings page above and click on the **General** tab. At the bottom of the **General** settings panel, the blue **View More Settings** link will take you immediately to your account's website settings.*

7.2 GENERAL

Settings in the general tab are fairly straightforward, and the labels are self explanatory. There are three things to note in this tab. First, near the top is a checkbox labeled **Enter full screen when starting or joining a meeting**. Most teachers I know like to have other applications open and visible when teaching a class, so not having Zoom automatically take up your whole screen suits that style better. Uncheck this box.

Second, you can do your eyes a great big favor by using **Dark mode** as much as possible on your computer. Dark mode for Zoom itself is accessed from the **Theme** section of the **General** tab. This will greatly reduce the amount of light, not just from the blue end of the spectrum, but all light coming from your computer. Dark mode is also available on your computer hardware. It can be set to run permanently, or if you want, only at certain times of day.

Theme

○ Light   ○ Dark   ⊙ Use System Setting

Reaction Skin Tone

View More Settings ☐

Dark mode from Zoom's settings

You can start with implementing dark mode after a certain point in the evening, say 18:00. I did, and pretty soon I started using dark mode all the time. I made the screenshots for this book in Light mode only because it's easier to look at them that way in print. Choosing **Use System Setting** for Zoom's dark mode will change Zoom according to what details you set on your computer.

The last important button in the **General** tab is the **View More Settings** button at the very bottom. That is the fastest way I know from within Zoom to go straight to your Zoom website account page.

7.3 VIDEO

Here you'll find a switch to turn on your computer's broadcast in HD. If you want to save bandwidth for some reason, this is an easy place to start.

If you feel a need to smooth out some wrinkles one day, try checking (√) the **Touch up my appearance** option. This will give you a slider that, when moved, gives your image a nice glow and smoothness with a special blur effect. Start a Zoom meeting with just yourself so that you can get a better view of how the effect looks. Before you try this, though, take a look at what I wrote above in the section on the Digital Stage about your lighting. Improving your stage lighting will drastically improve what your camera can send to your Zoom room. Note also that some related controls for touching up your appearance can be found in the Zoom **Studio Effects** panel. I'll talk about that later in the **Backgrounds & Filters** section.

I recommend that you turn off that **Always show video preview dialog when joining a video meeting**. As a teacher, I hope you aren't too much like some of our students and just stumble into class. I already know what I look like before I sit at my desk, and I use a waiting room anyway, so I find having to go through that video preview dialog a bit of a pain. Uncheck this.

Hide non-video participants makes for cleaner video recordings and makes it easier to see all active cameras if you're in a class where not many students turn them on. However, if someone with their camera turned off raises their hand or uses other reaction buttons, they won't be visible, so make sure you keep the participants list open for that.

I'm lucky to have a recently made computer with strong graphics capabilities so I can have up to 49 participants visible in my gallery view. This lets me see everyone without having to page between views. But it takes a lot of computer power and requires a strong and stable connection. If you haven't yet done so, you really should be using a LAN cable (Category 6e or better) when doing Zoom classes. If your setup can handle it, it's worth a try.

7.4 AUDIO

I've already made some mention of the audio controls you find in the application settings in Part III: The Digital Stage and Part IV: The Equipment Issue of this book. Take a look there for more information on what is important for your application audio settings.

7.5 CHAT

I was one of the many Zoom users who was initially confused about this part of the **Application** settings until I finally figured out that most of the controls here refer not to in-meeting chat, but instead to the chat that Zoom allows you to do with anyone in your Zoom contact list outside of meetings.

I talk a bit more about the difference in Part X: Zoom Chat and Channels.

7.6 BACKGROUND & FILTERS

I talked a bit already about some suggested uses for virtual backgrounds in the section "The Digital Stage," so take a look at that. Here I just want to mention that Zoom has included in its newer versions a series of filters you can add to your camera image, like little digital hats and hair bows.

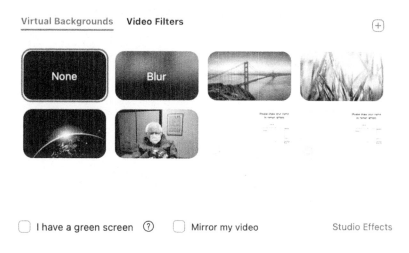

Zoom's virtual background screens, with a few custom screens uploaded.

Just below the background preview, you'll see a button labeled **Video Filters**. You'll find all kinds of filters in there. Your students might get a kick out of it for a change of pace. Then in the bottom right corner of the Backgrounds & Filters panel, there's a button labeled **Studio Effects** where you can find an array of fun effects that can give you a mustache or the pinkest lips this side of a Hollywood awards show. Knock yourself out; I'm not going to judge.

Studio Effects

All I want to say about this bit of the Zoom software is be careful of the checkbox at the top of that sliding panel; the one that says **Apply to all future meetings**. That's turned on by default, so if you just want to have some fun with your family, make sure you don't forget to uncheck that, or at least hit the **None** button for any effects you want to turn off, or else you might enter your next faculty meeting wearing strangely lush eyebrows and an avocado sprout on your head.

7.7 RECORDING

Optimize for 3rd party video editor should be checked if you intend to edit the class recording. The file size will go up when it's saved, and conversion time will increase, but you'll get the best possible file for editing video.

7.8 PROFILE

If you want to upgrade your Zoom account, click the button at the bottom, **View My Subscription**.

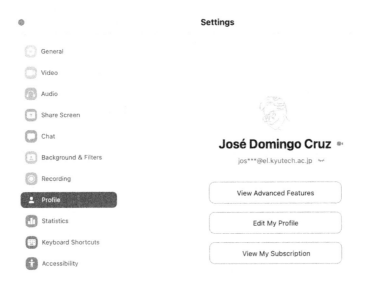

Access your Profile here.

Zoom isn't expensive software, considering what it can do and how important it is to our teaching. But really, most of what a paid account can get you, you can probably live without—except for the ability to hold unlimited-length meetings with up to 100 people. Until I was given a full Zoom account by one of my institutions, I was willing to pay to get that. Still, you can pay for that as you need it by foreseeing when you might want it and then getting an upgrade to your Zoom account for that month.

Beyond the first pro level, there are all kinds of feature levels you can pay for, and you can get a full-feature rundown on the webpage that button will take you to.

7.9 STATISTICS

If you are concerned or just curious about your bandwidth usage, you can see pretty much a real-time assessment of what your Zoom app is using for **CPU**, **Memory**, and **Bandwidth**. There are further tabs along the top of this panel for details on **Audio**, **Video**, and **Screen Sharing**. If you're a geek like me, you might find it interesting, but I doubt that most teachers would. I think the most important takeaway is that you can see how much data you send and receive.

There are plenty of pages on the internet that can tell you what Zoom is like for bandwidth usage, but here are some general figures.

In a group meeting or class using HD video, Zoom racks up about 1 to 1.3 gigabytes per hour for all of its uploads and downloads. The more people on the call, the more those figures go up. If everyone is dancing on their cameras, it goes up some more, and can go up further depending on what's being screen-shared. Not surprisingly, that is about the data rate for HD video streaming.

7.10 KEYBOARD SHORTCUTS

Learn as many of the keyboard shortcuts as you can. Apple long ago showed how keyboard shortcuts are the fastest way to execute any important computer command.

My favorites are the aforementioned **Show preferences** (Command-comma) and **Mute audio** (Control-Command-M). Press and hold the space key to unmute. Look through the various shortcuts for some that might make your workflow easier.

PRO TIP: *Click on the text of any of those shortcuts and you will be able to edit them to something else you prefer. Be careful though that you don't choose something that is already being used by the computer as a global keystroke, such as Command-S (for "save"). Zoom will not allow you to edit a shortcut to a keystroke sequence that is already being used by Zoom.*

7.11 ACCESSIBILITY

Here you can find the controls to resize your closed captioning text (which has a slider that shows you what the size of the captions will look like) and chat text (which lets you choose the percentage of size increase—120%, 150%, etc.).

If a student identifies as visually impaired, consider asking them to attend a private session during your office hours or other mutually agreeable time to test the settings and let you know what works best.

PART 8

SCREEN SHARING

Screen sharing is something you've probably done a few times already, but perhaps like a lot of Zoom's functions that you used this past year, you still have a few questions about how to do it better.

8.1 HOW CAN I MAKE MY ZOOM WINDOWS VISIBLE DURING A SCREEN SHARE?

When you're showing students how to do certain things in Zoom, it's much easier to show them where buttons are as opposed to describing them. If you're like me, a language teacher speaking in your second (or third) language, you know how especially taxing it can be trying to do tech help.

So, go to your website settings and look for **Show Zoom windows during screen share**, slide that toggle switch to the right, and restart Zoom. Go to the application settings, look under **Share Screen**, and you'll find a checkbox that starts, **Show my Zoom windows to other participants...**

Always show meeting control toolbar

Always show meeting controls during a meeting ⓥ

Show Zoom windows during screen share ⓥ

Turn on the screensharing button.

137

Check that, and all your Zoom windows will be visible to the students. This will make it much easier during a desktop screen share to show where meeting, scheduling, or preference buttons are and how to use them. The only caveat is that your computer has to have enough CPU and graphics power to actually be able to do it, regardless of whether you turn on the setting or not.

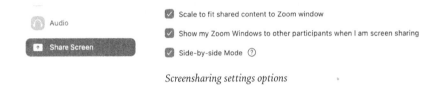

Screensharing settings options

8.2 WHAT CAN I USE THE IPHONE SHARING FUNCTIONS FOR?

On occasion, I have mounted my iPhone using my macrophotography accessories to a position over my desk. There I turn on the phone's camera function where it can view my hands as they display handwriting form (believe it or not, some of my students need remedial lessons on how to properly write Roman letters) or to show objects that I have or want to manipulate at my desk (think sewing or knitting).

If I have the iPhone connected wirelessly, I can show the students my desk or an alternate view of me as I teach; or sometimes in lighter moments, I have shown them around my renovated Japanese farmhouse.

Otherwise, the phone can show everything that its screen shows, so for example if you want to show the class how to use an app that helps them with their vocabulary learning, you can take a few minutes to show them how to actually do it on your own phone screen. What the phone can't do is share whatever sound it might be playing. That is not enabled during a screen share.

If you want to show what the phone can see and hear and play, bring the phone into the meeting as just another device, and when you want to, spotlight the phone's camera (and audio) so all the students will pay attention to it.

8.3 SHOULD I USE THE STEREO OR MONO OPTION FOR SHARING SOUND?

Use stereo if you need it specifically for music or performing arts; otherwise it's best to use less bandwidth with mono.

Also, if you do not have a stereo-capable microphone, and if your students do not have good enough speakers at their end to hear the difference, there might not be any point in using anything but mono.

8.4 WHAT DOES "OPTIMIZE FOR VIDEO CLIP" DO?

Zoom is a bit cryptic on what exactly this feature does, but they do state that you should check this only if you actually want to share a video clip. They also state that the bandwidth requirements go up. I surmise that the sharing function thus sends out a much higher frame rate over the server, so that the video being shared doesn't look jittery.

So, if you're only sharing mostly static images with a few changes in content as you type in different words, then you probably don't need to check that option. Not checking it will cut down on the amount of bandwidth your share will need to take, which is always an important consideration.

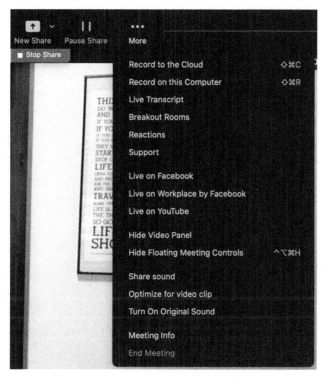

"Optimize for video clip" towards the bottom of the menu

---

*PRO TIP: If you forget to check the **Share sound** or **Optimize for video clip** before you begin a screen share, you don't need to start the share over again. Just go to the sharing toolbar and open the **More** menu on the far right, and you can activate either option while your share is still running.*

8.5 WHAT DOES THE GREEN ARROW NEXT TO THE SHARE BUTTON DO?

Why don't you click it and find out?

No, no, I'm just kidding. On the screen sharing toolbar next to the green **Share screen** button is an up arrow. The up arrows in Zoom often indicate the presence of a pop-up menu that will appear if you click on it.

That is where you can access some advanced sharing controls, such as for multiple sharing, who is allowed to share, and who can interrupt a share by starting a new share from their computer.

I would only set the last two options to *all participants* if necessary, and only when you are in a meeting where you know all the participants in it. Otherwise it's quite possible that a student in the middle of their presentation could be accidentally interrupted. That would be a shame if they were already nervous about it to begin with.

8.6 SHOULD I ALLOW MULTIPLE USERS TO SCREEN SHARE SIMULTANEOUSLY?

I haven't yet found myself needing to allow multiple students to share simultaneously, but I can imagine it could be useful to some teachers for say group presentations or debates. An archaeology class showing comparative techniques at two different dig sites might find the feature interesting; the possibilities stretch wide.

Do note that to make good use of multiple sharing, Zoom says that everyone should have multiple monitors, but it's actually not necessary. You would be wise to make sure your students know how to switch between the two available shares, if that is important to your lesson structure.

8.7 WHAT IS THE VANISHING PEN?

From about version 5.6.3 of Zoom, a very nice new feature was introduced that was part of the annotation features. Called the **Vanishing Pen** (VP), it works like any other annotation tool except that whatever is drawn with it vanishes in three seconds. This keeps your main screen share document or image from getting too cluttered with your highlighting.

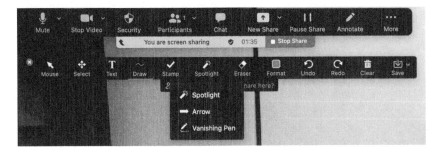

The Vanishing Pen tool

First, make sure that **Annotations** is turned on in your account's website settings. See also what I wrote in the **Security** section on being careful when **Annotation** is turned on.

When you call up annotations from the Screen Share toolbar, around the middle of the row of buttons will be **Spotlight.** Click that, and the **Vanishing Pen** option will appear underneath the previous choices of **Spotlight** and **Arrow**.

I tried it using my iPad and Apple Pencil using Mac OS Sidecar, and it worked well. Just take any document you want to share and use the VP with, and move it over to the iPad screen under **Sidecar**. When you choose what to share, select **Desktop 2**, which will be the iPad.

You can find out more about Sidecar here:
https://support.apple.com/guide/imac/sidecar-apde36aa0ecf/mac

8.8 WHY DOES MY AUDIENCE SOMETIMES SEE BLANK SPACES IN MY SHARE?

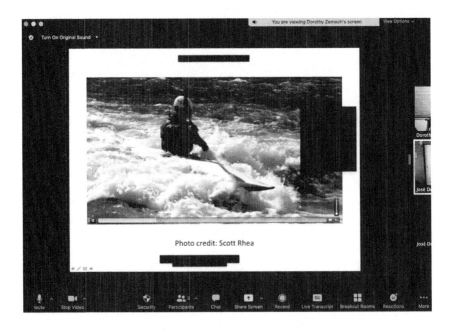

If your audience shows you a screenshot of your presentation having blank spaces in front of it, you probably have other windows—like the Zoom chat window—on top of your slide content.

The shape underneath the picture of the kayak is clearly the same shape as the Zoom screenshare toolbar, and the box to the right is probably the Zoom chat. So, be careful of anything being on top of your slides.

8.9 CAN I MAKE THE TEXT IN THE SHARED BROWSER WINDOW BIGGER?

Take a look at my recommendations I make later in section 8.12 about sharing windows with a horizontal, NOT a vertical orientation.

Basically, make sure before you start sharing that the window you want to show is rectangular in a landscape orientation. I suggest a ratio of 9:5.

If not, while the text might look sufficiently legible to you, remember that students with less powerful internet connections can't see the text as well, and if you scroll the screen too quickly, their view of your share might not refresh fast enough for them to see what you're talking about.

So keep your share windows as small as possible; the smaller the window, the larger the relative size of the text will be on your students' computers.

8.10 HOW CAN I SEE MORE STUDENTS WHILE I'M SHARING?

When Zoom starts your screen share, it reduces the speaker view or gallery view of the classroom to a small strip of that usually orients itself to the right side of your monitor. You can move that camera grid.

If you haven't noticed them, there are a series of buttons at the top of the reduced camera display grid. They switch how many cameras you can view in the grid at a time. From the left, they go: **camera off - speaker/spotlighted camera - gallery strip view - gallery grid view**.

In strip view, you can see more students by clicking the pagination arrows at the bottom or top of the strip. If you choose grid view, you can make the grid a little bigger by dragging on the handles at the bottom corners. **Grid view** is my recommendation.

8.11 HOW CAN I MAKE THE IMAGE OF THE PERSON SHARING THE SCREEN BIGGER FOR A RECORDING?

Make sure that you are in **active speaker view** during screen share (that's the button with the thick single bar, second from the left), then look at the corners of the active speaker box and drag it to enlarge.

Note that if you use this option, the meeting recording video will have an exaggerated width to accommodate the enlarged active speaker image. Doing this on your host screen will not change the image size on attendee computers.

8.12 WHY DO MY VIDEO RECORDINGS WITH SHARED SCREENS HAVE A VERTICAL ORIENTATION?

At some point in the recording, you were probably sharing windows that were taller than they were wide. Zoom will try to fit all of a window's content into the recording, even if it was only for a few seconds. Thus, you should plan ahead what you want to share and make sure that the dimensions of the windows you want to show are in generally a horizontal format. However, if you plan on enlarging the active speaker view, you should keep that in mind too, as that will also alter the eventual dimensions of your recording.

It's best to remember that just like sharing, recording a Zoom meeting is all about conveying information, and if the windows you are sharing have text that is too small to read in your meeting window, the attendees will begin to lose focus.

Before you start a class, prepare all the windows you will share and resize them to roughly the proportions of your own monitor, so in a horizontal orientation, roughly something like 5:3 (5 segments wide, 3 segments tall). This will look much nicer on most computer screens than sharing windows that remain in a vertical orientation. Do some test recordings of any window arrangements if you want to try to see how they look.

8.13 WHAT IS THE VIDEO SHARING OPTION LIKE?

It functions adequately, and if you have no other option, it will do well enough to play a recorded video. But its functions are limited, and you are probably used to the built-in video player that your computer already has.

I prefer to simply open a video in my Mac's QuickTime player and share that. On Windows 10, the default video player is called "Groove Music."

8.14 WHAT DO YOU USE THE "COMPUTER AUDIO" OPTION FOR?

Very simply, this is like any other screen share except that you won't be sharing anything visually. But everything your computer is doing with its audio will be audible to your audience; that includes ALL alert and background sounds. The Zoom meeting window and its controls will respond as it normally does. The only thing that tells you a screen share is happening is the green indicator at the top of the meeting window, and the red **Stop Share** button next to it.

This option is good if all you want to do is share audio and still want to appear in a large screen to the students—say, if you were playing a song and showing how to play the same chords on a guitar. If you want to show a bit of text on a page while you have a voice read it over, you're still better off with a regular screen share of the text you want to show, with the **Share sound** checkbox checked and the sound playing from an mp3 player on your computer.

8.15 HOW DO I USE THE "CONTENT FROM 2D CAMERA" OPTION?

This will allow you to take any camera that interfaces with your computer via USB or HDMI and can be recognized by Zoom's camera selector to be the share source. If you have an advanced tabletop overheard camera on your desk, it might be interesting. Most people who have a DSLR available to Zoom can use that to show images via that camera.

You can also use software like Snap Camera to put filters on the face of the person in the camera. I found that amusing for about 2-3 minutes, but I haven't used it much since the cat-lawyer incident. I doubt I want to use it much in my classes. My students already don't take me seriously enough. (See https://globalnews.ca/news/7631634/cat-lawyer-zoom-filter/)

But if, say, you are a zoology professor and you have a GoPro camera hooked up into a giraffe pen, your timing might be lucky enough one day to show a live birthing procedure to your students who tuned in that day.

8.16 HOW DOES "SLIDES AS VIRTUAL BACKGROUND" WORK?

Here's an option in the **Advanced** screen sharing menu that I find very useful: using one of your PowerPoint or Keynote slideshows as a virtual background (VB).

This was a good addition to Zoom's feature set. It makes it easier to have your image visible to the audience and the Zoom recording without having to waste a lot of screen space under your camera view, because when you use slides as a VB, your image is visible inside the slide set itself.

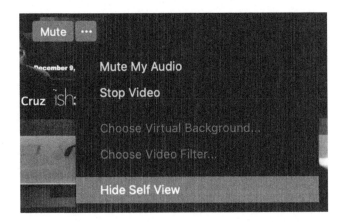

It's also still visible above the entire slideshow as a **Self View**. If you find the self view distracting, you can turn it off by hovering your cursor over it to reveal a three-dot button. Click that button and midway down the menu that appears you will find the item **Hide Self View**. Your image within the slide set is a resizable and movable. If you don't like that effect either, you can turn it off by clicking on the three-dot button next to the slide counter and choosing **Split Video from Slides**.

If you want to bring the camera back inside the slides, go back to the three-dot button and menu option will then become **Merge**.

Note that your slides will lose their ability to show any of your nicely created transitions, or play any video or audio you embedded in them, so be careful that you re-edit your slides if any of your explanations rely on those elements.

8.17 HOW SHOULD I USE THE "PORTION OF SCREEN" OPTION?

This is another very useful option in the Advanced sharing menu. The name is fairly self-explanatory. So it's pretty easy to understand when you choose this option what the green box means when it appears. The image that is displayed to your audience is everything that is in the interior of the box. You can resize the borders of the box by dragging on the sides or corners.

During a resize, the box color will turn orange, which means that whatever is being displayed will remain static while Zoom re-buffers the video image. Sometimes due to a poor connection or a heavy CPU load, the border will turn orange even if you are not resizing it. You will then sometimes hear Zoom make an alert sound that sounds quite appropriately like the grunt an uncooperative dog would make when it is pulling in the other direction of your leash. That indicates that you still have to wait for Zoom to finish re-buffering before you can do anything, and that includes clicking on anything inside the screen share. When the box turns green again, Zoom has finished re-buffering.

I like to use **Portion of screen** when I have a few different separate windows that I want to show quickly in sequence, and I don't want to waste time starting and stopping for a new share every time I want to show a different window or application. Instead, before class I make them all the same size and stack them on top each other, and then use my application switcher to get the app window I want frontmost. I talk more about this in Part XIII on using Zoom for other educational purposes.

8.18 CAN I SHARE FROM MY IPAD?

It's not something I recommend that you do a lot, but if you have an iPad and you're in a pinch, like your main computer goes down, you can still use your iPad as an emergency hosting computer.

Most other issues for using an iPad aren't so hard to figure out. Remember that you cannot do breakout rooms from a tablet, but you can share content. Still, sharing can be quite unintuitive because of how the controls appear, so here are some basic points.

In the screenshot, the share button is still the familiar green, but is now situated near the top right of the iPad screen, and is labeled **Share Content.**

The Share Content button in the upper right

Click **Share Content** and you'll get the following choices. Except for the first two options, the majority are for sharing files from various cloud services such as Dropbox or, as you can see in the next screen, Google Drive. The first choice is what we will look at here: sharing your **Screen**.

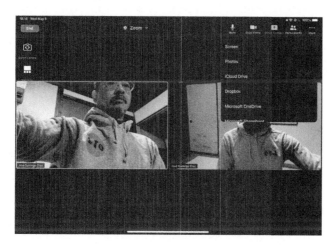

The Sharing menu

Upon clicking **Screen**, you'll get the mostly dark screen you see next, except for the buttons for **Start Broadcast** and **Microphone**

Off. This is where some of the terminology can be confusing. Think of **Start Broadcast** as meaning "Start showing your screen to the meeting." Click that, and from that point on, anything that appears on your iPad screen will appear in the meeting.

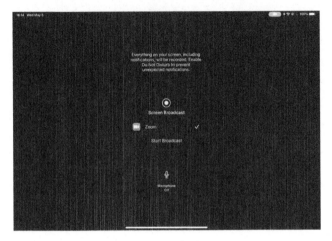

Start Broadcast

Microphone off is actually a button. If you tap that button, it will turn red, indicating that your microphone is live to the audience as well. Once you tap **Start Broadcast**, a 3-second countdown will begin, and the circles above the label, **Screen Broadcast**, will start to flash and turn red. You might think that something is being recorded, but nothing is. It's only an indicator that your iPad is being shared.

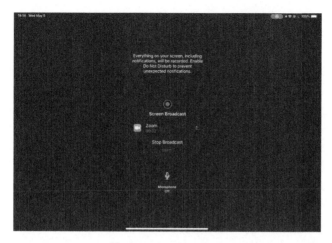

The Screen Broadcast screen

Tap anywhere on the gray area outside of the broadcast controls and the **Sharing screen** warning appears. From here you can engage the normal swipe up to enter the normal iPad interface, where you can show anything that appears on the tablet's screen back to the Zoom meeting—photos, movies, a slide show, whatever.

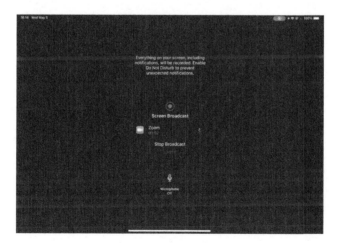

Stop broadcast button

The red dot that appears in the iPad's top right corner is an indicator that you are still sharing your iPad screen.

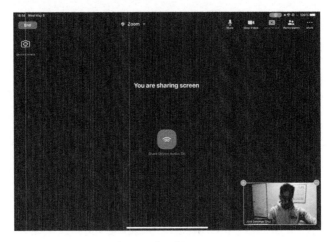

A screen share in progress

Tap that red button and you will see the dialog box below asking if you want to stop the screen share.

Ending the screenshare

If you take a look at the original **Share** options, you'll find at the bottom the option for sharing a whiteboard with your audience, which is nice to have.

I have to say, I think Zoom can clean up this interface a bit to make it a little less confusing, by eliminating that "You are sharing your screen" panel, relabeling the buttons, and not using words like "broadcast." Still, if you log on with your normal Zoom account credentials on your iPad, you can host a couple of classes in an emergency. However, I certainly don't think this is anything I would want to do for anymore than a couple of days until I get a chance to fix my computer.

8.19 CAN I STOP ZOOM FROM RESIZING MY WINDOW?

When I first started using Zoom, I found it a little disorienting the first time I shared my screen and Zoom resized it to take up my entire monitor area. Zoom often changes screen sizes for different meeting events. I don't like having my chosen window size changed, no matter how much the software designer thinks it's for my convenience. So here are the two places where you can control how Zoom manipulates your window sizes. They're pretty self-explanatory.

Starting or joining a meeting: Application settings>>General>> Uncheck **Enter full screen when starting or joining a meeting** (second from the top)

Screen sharing: Application settings>>Share screen>> **Window size when screen sharing**. Of the three radio buttons at the top, I prefer **Maintain current size**.

If you do find that your Zoom window goes fullscreen, you can immediately get it down to a smaller size by double clicking anywhere on the Zoom meeting camera area that isn't already an active area, such as a clickable link or button.

8.20 CAN I MAKE MY SLIDESHOW NOT GO FULLSCREEN WHEN I SHARE?

I would bet that the most shared software by not just teachers in Zoom meetings but by almost anyone is PowerPoint, Keynote, or some other slideshow system.

One issue that came up is that slide presentation software was designed to be used in classrooms on a projector, so that when a user started an actual presentation, it was actually handy for the slideshow to take the entire screen, so that it could be easily viewed from a lectern one or two meters away.

During remote classes, however, it's quite inconvenient, as you want to be able to see your notes and other things that are on your computer. And this isn't a problem with Zoom; this time it's with the presentation software. But I get questions about this often enough that I thought I'd make an exception and talk about this in detail.

Keynote (Mac): The newest version of Keynote makes it very easy to play slideshow in a separate window. There is now a button to the right of the **Play** button at the top of the Keynote window that says **Play in a Window**. If you can't see the **Play in a Window**

button, you might have made the Keynote window too small, and if you make it a little bigger, that will provide enough space for it to appear.

PowerPoint (Mac or Windows): For PowerPoint, the instructions are essentially the same on either platform. In the PowerPoint window, look at the top of the window in the "ribbon," click on the **Slide Show** tab, then look for **Set Up Slide Show**. That will open a small window where you will find a section called **Show Type**. In there, you want to click the second radio button labeled **Browsed by an individual (window)**. Doing so will change the setting only for that particular slideshow, so don't forget to change it for all the slideshows you want to show this way.

PART 9

BREAKOUT ROOMS

I remember hearing early on from some of my peers here in Japan who were being forced to work with Microsoft Teams or Google Meet or some other videoconferencing system the university had already contracted for long before emergency remote teaching. They would complain about several things on those platforms that made me grateful I didn't have to be in their shoes. But the biggest thing that stood out for me was how they had to try to work without breakout rooms (BORs).

Most of the university instructors I know are language teachers, and almost all of them who couldn't use Zoom wanted it primarily for its breakout rooms. Things have progressed since then, with Teams and Google Meet now having BORs, and almost anyone who uses videoconferencing considers BORs indispensable. I do as well; I couldn't do my fluency-training based language classes without them.

BORs are where Zoom really runs out ahead of the pack.

9.1 HOW DO I ACTIVATE BREAKOUT ROOMS IN MY ACCOUNT?

If you start a meeting as the host, and you don't immediately see the breakout rooms (BORs) button at the right hand side of the window tool bar between the **Record** and **Reactions** buttons, then you'll need to visit your website Zoom account.

Login and go to the **Settings** page, and in the **Meetings** tab, scroll about three-quarters of the way down the page for section titled **In Meeting (Advanced)**.

The second setting from the top of that section will be a switch that lets you activate the BORs. Move it to the right. It will turn blue, and the next time you host a meeting on the same account, you will see the BORs button where it should be.

9.2 DOES ZOOM ALLOW USERS TO SELF-SELECT BREAKOUT ROOMS?

When they released version 5.3 around October 2020, Zoom provided a new way for users to enter BORs.

Previously, users could only be assigned either automatically to a random BOR, or the host could move users in and out of rooms manually. Now a room host has a third choice when they click the BOR button in the window toolbar: **Let Participant choose room**. This allows users to choose the room where they want to go.

When the host chooses the self-select option and opens BORs, the meeting members will see a BOR button on their own meeting toolbar. Members can then click it and will see the list of BORs either numbered by default or as they might have been renamed by the host.

To the extreme right of the room name is a button that says **Join** for Windows users, and for Mac users, a number indicating the current population number of the room. If you see the **Join** button, click it and then confirm that you want to enter the room. For Macs, hover your cursor over the population number, and that number will turn into the **Join** button.

Make sure that all students in your class have an updated version of Zoom, or they will not be able to choose their own room. You as the host, however, can still move students manually into a BOR.

9.3 HOW DO I RENAME BREAKOUT ROOMS?

Immediately after you choose the number of BORs and the user entry mode (automatic, manual, or self-select), you will be shown a panel where the room numbers are listed. Each listed room will have a **Rename** button to the right of the Room number, which if clicked, allows the room host to enter a new name.

Choose your room name well and watch for typos, as after BORs begin, rooms cannot be renamed.

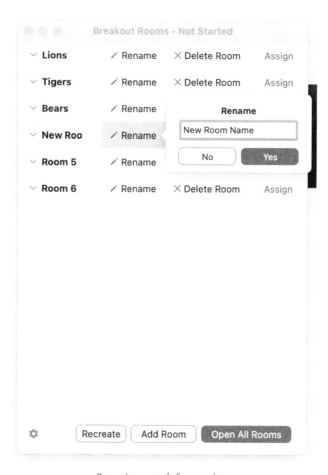

Renaming rooms before opening

9.4 CAN USERS MOVE BETWEEN ROOMS?

After BORs have started and meeting members have entered self-selected rooms, they can move easily between rooms by once again clicking on the **Breakout Rooms** button at the bottom of their toolbar and choosing a different BOR to enter.

Choosing the room is slightly different depending on your computer platform. On a Windows PC, the **Join** button is immediately visible upon opening the dialog box. On a Mac, the **Join** button only appears when you hover your cursor over your chosen room's population number on the right.

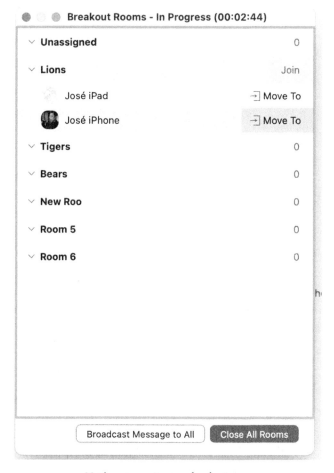

Moving someone to a new breakout room

In any type of BOR, users also have the option of clicking the blue **Leave Room** button that will appear to replace the red **Leave** button. This will allow them to re-enter the main meeting room. Some users may do this if they feel they need to consult with the meeting host for more information.

9.5 CAN I HAVE STUDENTS MOVED INTO BREAKOUT ROOMS AS SOON AS I OPEN THEM?

Teachers sometimes wish they could get students to enter breakout rooms more quickly. Even with an energetic class, students can sometimes take up to 15-20 seconds to just push the button that asks them to join a BOR. That may not seem like much, but in some of my classes, the students are in their rooms for only three minutes maximum, so that can be a sizable chunk of the total time.

You can choose to have students moved automatically anytime after you start BORs. See the screenshot. After you choose the number of rooms you want and choose the option for move automatically, click the gear button at the bottom left bottom of the BOR room window and in the dialog box that appears, click the checkbox third from the top: **Automatically move all...**

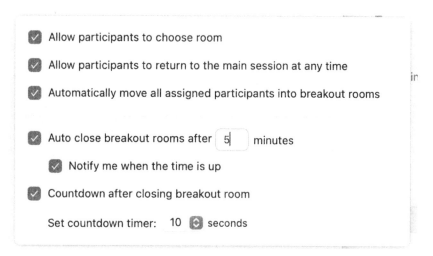

Breakout room settings

If you choose to allow students to move between rooms (the checkbox at the top), they can still do so. The option to make students join automatically only forces them into a room at the beginning.

9.6 IS THERE A WAY TO GET BETTER RANDOMIZATION OF MEMBERS IN BREAKOUT ROOMS?

In language education, many classes like to use BORs to send students to do pair or group work.

I like to set up a series of BORs where I want students to be paired with a different random partner every time. Yet like others, I find that some pairs are repeated or that I don't feel the pairs of groups are sufficiently randomized, even though I've recreated the rooms.

I found however that I can get better randomization of members if I recreate the rooms twice: first at a number that is less than half of the number that I really want (say, three instead of seven), and then recreate a second time at the number of rooms I really want. This I find will sufficiently get Zoom to move the students around the BORs to make sure that they get to work with in as many different groupings as possible.

9.7 ARE THERE BETTER WAYS TO COMMUNICATE WITH STUDENTS IN BREAKOUT ROOMS?

Teachers often wish they could easily communicate with students they've sent to BORs. Unfortunately with the word "easily" being part of the question, the answer involves varying levels of difficulty. Zoom's internal functions make screen sharing, chat, and other functions for any member of a meeting limited to the actual room they are in. Whether it be the main room or a breakout, a host or participant can use Zoom's functions only there.

Within Zoom's own feature set is the ability for the host to send one-way messages to all BORs, but that's it. You can access it at the bottom of the BOR list, **Broadcast Message to All**. But messages can't be focused into any particular room, and more importantly there is no way for students to answer in chat. I found that when I used it, many students didn't see my BOR broadcasts as often as I thought they did, because the chat appears in small print at the top of the room for only a limited time.

At this point in Zoom's development, for a user in one room of a meeting to communicate with a different room, separate software is required.

Some instructors regularly use a group chat in Skype or some other software to allow users to have one central location where they can talk altogether while still in separate rooms. Other teachers use Google's Jamboard or a Google doc shared with all students in the class to draw pictures or show text that all users can see while they work in BORs. This has one disadvantage, in that to use Zoom and Google docs and perhaps keep open another web browser window to do all the work that the session might require might be difficult on a computer with a small monitor or on a phone.

9.8 CAN I COMBINE USING ZOOM WITH SOCIAL MEDIA?

I have had some success using Zoom with Facebook. I would continue using it except that my main university forbids me from having any kind of social media contact with my students.

When I did use it, I put all my students into a private Facebook group early on in the class. They could then communicate with each other using the Messenger software on their phones while doing their classwork on their main computer. This might, however, be a problem with those special students who find themselves for whatever reason with only a phone as their single internet device for all their schoolwork. But then, such students always need special attention, no matter what ideas you try. Phones were not meant to be used as primary classroom devices.

However, if you are sure all of your students have both a regular computer as well as an internet-capable device like a phone or a tablet, they can have Messenger open on the smaller device while they attend a Zoom class on their main computer.

9.9 CAN ZOOM LIVESTREAM TO SOCIAL MEDIA?

One place where a private Facebook group really works well with a Zoom class, however, is in the relatively new function that Zoom has for doing a livestream of a Zoom meeting into a Facebook group or personal page, or a YouTube channel.

If you go to the website settings for your pro-level Zoom account, you will find the settings for **Allow livestreaming of meetings** under **In meeting (Advanced)**. You can switch it on for Facebook and YouTube and other streaming services.

Livestreaming options

Facebook is better for this particular purpose as you can have better social media functions that might be useful in a class. Once you have the setting enabled, you'll find a new button in your toolbar to the right of the **Reactions** button labeled **More**. Click that to open the choices you selected for livestreaming. Click your venue of choice and follow their instructions for how to get the stream started. Facebook has a very simple system that shouldn't challenge anyone who knows enough to manage Zoom.

In a Zoom livestream, anything that appears in the meeting window will appear in the livestream. So all of your audio and shared screens will be available to view and hear via a browser to anyone in any BOR.

But how do the students communicate back to you? Well, the livestream appears as a post in Facebook, so if the students in BORs need to, they can comment under that livestream post, which the instructor can then see. Because they can hear you, you can choose to respond either in text as part of the comment thread or in voice over the livestream.

Any livestreams sent to a Facebook group will be recorded and can be viewed later, so they make a good archive of an entire class if you wish to use it that way. Any chat done as a comment thread under the livestream has the great advantage of being given a clickable timestamp. After the livestream is turned into a recording, the comment timestamps can be clicked and the video will jump to the exact moment that the comment was sent to the thread (which is sometimes up to a minute after the writer thought to start making the comment).

The students' faces will also be recorded, so you should make that clear to the students and keep a tight watch on the privacy settings for your Facebook group. You might also want to make sure with your institution that doing anything that involves recording student images and voices like this doesn't violate school rules.

If you can't use Facebook or livestreams with your students, you might want to check if you are still allowed to use some kind of group messaging app with your class.

9.10 DO YOU HAVE ANY OTHER TIPS WHEN USING BREAKOUT ROOMS?

Here are a few miscellaneous tips.

TELL STUDENTS TO UNMUTE BEFORE THEY ENTER THE BORS

I use high-speed fluency practices in my English classes, so my BORs are often very short—two or sometimes only one minute long. In such cases, if a student takes 10-15 seconds of fumbling just to unmute themselves when they enter the BOR, that is up to 25% of the time.

So I tell my students to unmute just *before* I start the BORs. That way when they enter the BOR, they are ready to start doing the fluency practice right away. Use the **Ask All to Unmute** command found in the **Meeting** menu.

GET READY TO LEAVE TO THE NEXT BOR AS SOON AS YOU ENTER ONE

When I go to check in on students' progress in BORs, I see if I can give them some advice and encouragement. In a normal physical classroom, I would leave on that note and move over to the next group in the room, but in Zoom there's that awkward few seconds after you say goodbye and then you have to fumble about with the BOR control panel as you check on the next room you want to visit.

If you want to cut that down, use the few seconds as soon as you enter the room and need to listen to students to simultaneously start setting the button to push to leave. Now when you say "Bye," you can hit the **Join** button to leave for the next room you want to visit at the same time.

PART 10

ZOOM CHAT AND CHANNELS

Note that Zoom has two types of chat: one for in-meeting, and the other for chatting with people in your Zoom contact list outside of meetings. Most of the customization options in your **Application** settings control out-of-meeting chat.

The Chat tab, third button from the top upper right

At the top of the Zoom window next to the **Home** tab you'll find the **Chat** tab. This is different from the in-meeting chat. Zoom provides this messaging function to work like Facebook messenger or Skype.

Personally, I don't find Zoom messaging terribly engaging, although that's not because it's missing any important features. It's just that I already use FB Messenger or sometimes LINE. You probably already do most of your instant messaging on your own favorite software. Moreover, I don't have a large contact list of friends registered in my Zoom, and I don't need to have them there, as I can conveniently call them into Zoom meetings just by sending them a URL via whatever chat software I already use with them. Going through the steps required to add them to my Zoom contact list just so I can text chat with them there seems superfluous.

On the other hand, if you are running small private classes and you don't have access to an LMS, and you don't necessarily want to bring these students into your Facebook friend list just so can make group chats with them, Zoom Channels might be one way you have to get around this problem.

You'll find Channels inside the **Contacts** tab. After you have added friends to your Zoom account, you can then organize them into Channels, often called "Groups" in other software. In a channel you can do group chats, send files to members (e.g., assignment PDFs), and you can leave audio messages for each other.

Best of all, once a channel is created, starting your weekly meeting is as simple as clicking the start meeting icon. As long as all users are sitting at their computers on time with their Zoom running, they will be called into a meeting. I did this with a small group of students back in 2020. What we didn't do in Zoom for communicating we could do in a private Facebook group that I used as a quasi-LMS. It worked so well that I thought I would try to use it for all my university classes.

I didn't account for pushback, however, from several fronts. Japan generally has a leery view of Facebook, and young Japanese, like many young people around the world, consider Facebook as the social media that their parents use. The kicker, though, was that one university did not want any of their instructors having any kind of social media contact with their students.

10.1 HOW DO I REGISTER CONTACTS?

To use Channels, first you'll need to add people to your Zoom contact list. Click the **Contact** tab at the top of the Zoom window and you'll see a small plus "+" button next to the buttons for **Contacts/Channels**. Select **Invite a Zoom Contact** and a dialogue box appears where you can enter your friend's Zoom email. Click **Invite** and your friend will receive a notification asking them to confirm it.

Invite Zoom contacts here

If the friend asks you where it was sent, tell them to look inside their Zoom account's out-meeting chat window for a "contact request" from you, and to confirm it by clicking **Accept**. Once they become your contact, you can start moving them into a Channel.

Invite to Zoom

Email Address

Enter email address

If this user accepts your request, your profile information (including your status) will be visible to this contact. You can also meet and chat with this contact.

Cancel   Invite

10.2 HOW DO I MAKE CHANNELS?

Go to the **Contacts** tab in the Zoom window and click the **Add** button ("+"). In the pop-up menu that appears, second from the top you'll find the menu item for **Create a Channel**. A dialogue box will appear, allowing you to name the new channel and make choices about the group activity. You can edit any of these later. When you're done, click **Create Channel**. It will now appear in your **Channels** list inside the **Contacts** tab.

From there you can start adding members or performing other management tasks by clicking on the three-dot button to the right of the channel name.

Create a Channel

Channel Name

State Uni Wed 1st period

Channel Type

○ Public Anyone in your organization can find and join

◉ Private Invited members in your organization can join

Privacy

☑ External users can be added

    ◉ By all channel members

    ○ By members in your organization

Add Members(Optional)

Name, channel, or email address

Manage Posting Permissions

◉ Everyone

○ Admin only

○ Admin, plus specific people

Cancel   Create Channel

The Create a Channel settings

If you wish to start a chat with the entire channel, click the chat button immediately to the right of the Channel name. For a video meeting, the button is to the right of the one for chat. To talk with individuals in the channel, hover your cursor over their name that appears in the Channel member list on the right and click the chat or video button for that person.

10.3 HOW CAN I BETTER USE THE IN-MEETING CHATBOX?

While I'm not overly enthusiastic about it, in-meeting chat can be a very handy place for a few different functions as long as you know how to navigate it. Of course it's basically just chat, like Skype or Facebook Messenger, but it can also be slightly harder to use because during a meeting your attention is more focused on the video and audio of the meeting.

One of the first things I would recommend to improve the Zoom chat is to make the chat text size easier to see by enlarging it. You'll find that under **Accessibility** in the application settings. There you'll find a pop-up menu to enlarge the text up to double its original size. Above that menu is where you can use a slider to increase the size of closed captions. You could even reduce the size slightly, although I have no idea why you would want to do that; Zoom's chat text is already so tiny, my old man eyes struggle to see the text easily.

You might be wondering why a chat setting is in the **Accessibility** settings. I certainly did. But it turns out that Zoom's chat settings are for controlling the software's messaging functions, not its in-meeting chat.

I suppose that's OK, as Zoom's in-meeting chat system is pretty basic and doesn't need a lot of explanation, so it doesn't have a lot of settings that you can change. I have listed some tactics in the following sections, however, that should help you go a little faster with chat.

10.4 WHAT'S A FASTER WAY TO RESPOND PRIVATELY IF I'M IN A LARGE MEETING?

The largest Zoom meetings I find myself in aren't that large, maybe 100 people or so, but with anything over 40 participants, it can get pretty tough to navigate the chatbox if you want to send an acquaintance a private message. I used to scroll the whole list of participants to choose their name.

But a faster way is to just look at the direct chat message they actually wrote and then click on their name and that will tell the chat that you want to directly message that person. You can confirm that the message will go to them directly because it says "Direct Message" in red. If you click on any person's name in the running chat, that will turn the text entry field into a direct message with that person.

You can also click on the name list and as the pop-up menu of names appear, start typing on your keyboard the name of the person, and Zoom will use that as a find prompt and start narrowing the number of names that can fit that string of letters you just typed. Once you narrow down the list enough and can see the name you want, click on it and again, you're ready to direct message that person.

10.5 CAN I AUTOMATICALLY HAVE MY MEETING CHATS SAVED?

Certainly. Go to the website settings page for your account and in your browser find function, type *Chat*. This should tell your browser to go to that part of the page with that occurrence of the text string. There you will see the entire section of settings pertaining to Chat.

Look a little below to find the setting for **Auto saving chats**. Slide it to the right to turn it on. All files like chats, transcripts, and audio video recordings are arranged by date and time per meeting in the Zoom folder inside your computer's documents folder.

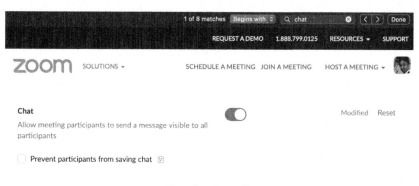

Save chats (or not!)

10.6 SHOULD I ALLOW MY STUDENTS TO ENGAGE IN PRIVATE CHAT?

I used to think that I didn't want my students to be able to use private chat over Zoom. I thought they might use it to distract themselves from what they should be doing, or that there might be too many ways for one student with a crush on another to make the latter feel uncomfortable, so I turned it off for all my classes in 2020.

Then I spoke to my colleague Curtis Hart Kelly, who is an expert in social aspects of the classroom, and he said that reducing students' ability to strengthen social bonds would do more harm than good overall.

Yes, there might be possible abuse of the chat, but being able to backchannel or front channel about the matter at hand—i.e., my lesson—is something we have to trust our students to use well as long as we teach them how to do so. Curtis convinced me that I should give it a try in the other direction this year, and so far I haven't encountered any problems.

10.7 HOW DO I MAKE CHAT BECOME A POP-OUT WINDOW?

When you access chat on Zoom for the very first time, the **Chat** window appears by sliding out to the side of the meeting window. If you have the **Participants** window concurrently visible, **Chat** will appear below it with a thin gray line separating them.

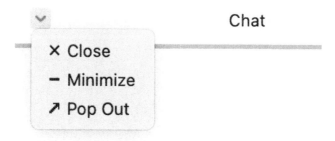

Chat window options

At the top corner of either one is a small down-arrow button that you can click to tell either window how to appear on your desktop during a meeting. **Pop Out** is the last option on the list. If the chat is in pop-up mode, you can get it to merge with the main meeting window again by clicking on the three-dot button at its lower right, and choosing the last option on that list, **Merge to Meeting Window.**

10.8 WHY DOES MY CHAT BECOME A POP-UP WINDOW WHEN I MAKE MY MEETING FULL SCREEN?

Because that's what Zoom thinks you want. You asked for a full screen meeting window, so they gave precedence to making the meeting window as big as possible, which meant making both the chat and participants windows appear as pop-ups.

There is a workaround, however, if you want your participants and chat windows to stay to the side of the meeting window but still get as big a meeting window as possible.

Simply use the window resize controls by dragging at the corners of the window to the extreme corners of your monitor. That will keep Zoom in normal window mode, and the participants and chat windows will stay where they are. It's a bit more of a bother to resize the window, but if keeping the chat window at the side is important to you, it's not that bad.

PRO TIP: Keep an eye on your Zoom folder if you are in the habit of autosaving chats or recording separate audio. You'd be surprised how quickly the Zoom documents folder will build up with files. Check to see what you can toss out if you don't need it anymore. One hour of recorded video can use up to one gigabyte of disk space.

10.9 CAN ZOOM REALLY DO AUTOMATIC SPEAKER TRANSCRIPTION NOW?

Yes, it can, and surprisingly well, but with a couple of limitations. First you have to enable the function in your accounts website settings. Search the settings for the switch to turn on **Closed Captioning**. While you're there, you may as well turn on the options for showing the captions on the side-panel, and allow users to **Save Captions**.

Closed captioning

Allow host to type closed captions or assign a participant/third party device to add closed captions

☑ Enable live transcription service to show transcript on the side panel in-meeting

Save Captions

Allow participants to save fully closed captions or transcripts

Closed captioning settings

As of this writing, the AI that does automatic transcriptions is limited to English speech, and you can initiate it only from paid or institutional-level Zoom accounts.

Nonetheless, it is quite impressive in understanding natural speech and even does a better job than Google's or Microsoft's automatic transcription, as Zoom's algorithm attempts to punctuate. I'd say that its accuracy is about 98%, so certainly adequate for meetings and presentations among high-level speakers and even most classes. English as a Second or Foreign Language classes might be a different matter, depending on how much the teacher needs such transcriptions to be accurate. Also, be aware that the accuracy is reduced if you have a sub-optimal audio environment or are not using a good quality microphone. See for yourself how it works in your setup by doing a live test before you use it in class.

I'll be using it for my classes, as giving my students opportunities to reinforce their aural comprehension with visual input should be useful. Unfortunately, in neither the cloud recording nor the local video recording version of a transcribed meeting are the closed captions saved in the video recording; a shame, that. But the transcripts that are saved as .vtt files do have timestamps within the text.

For languages other than English, Zoom has no ability to do automatic transcription, so there you'll have to do manual transcription. You can either choose to have one of your participants do the manual transcription or do it yourself. The person doing manual transcription must be working from a desktop or notebook computer.

I would have loved to have had a full transcript of my professor's lectures back in my university days. It would have left me free to write more useful notes to myself, if I knew that I also had a complete record of the stuff we covered in class.

The transcriptions appear in a small window, initially at the bottom of the meeting, but that can be moved by each user where they like it. For mobile devices, the transcription window can't be moved. You can download the transcription text once the meeting is over; unfortunately, although *during* a meeting the transcription window indicates who said or typed what, that information is not recorded in the downloaded transcription in the .vtt file.

Be careful that you (the host) stop transcription completely BEFORE you end the meeting or recording. You do that by returning to the "Live Transcript" button on the meeting toolbar, clicking it and clicking the blue **Disable Auto-Transcription** button. If you forget to turn off the transcription before you end the meeting, I have found that sometimes not all of the transcript is saved to the .vtt file.

Advanced cloud recording settings

   ☐ Add a timestamp to the recording ⑦

   ☑ Display participants' names in the recording

   ☑ Record thumbnails when sharing ⑦

   ☐ Optimize the recording for 3rd party video editor ⑦

   ☑ Audio transcript ⑦

   ☐ Save panelist chat to the recording ⑦

   ☐ Save poll results shared during the meeting/webinar ⑦

Audio transcript in cloud recordings

To enable saving of the .vtt files for cloud recordings, you have to go to the website settings and in the **Recording** tab, look for the section labeled **Advanced cloud recording settings** and check the option for **Audio transcript**.

PRO TIP: *If you are the transcriber for a meeting, I have found some success using manual transcription with the voice dictation function on my Mac. I've done it with both Japanese and English. It takes some getting used to, but I know I can speak faster than I can type, and with practice you get better at knowing when to hit the return key to send the packets of voice transcription to the Zoom window.*

10.10 WHAT ARE SOME ALTERNATIVES TO THE ZOOM WHITEBOARD?

I tried the Zoom Whiteboard when I first used Zoom back in April 2020. Zoom was maybe at about version 4.5. I tried it again recently to see if it had changed much since then, and in my opinion it hasn't changed much, so my reasons for not wanting to use it still remain.

I find it clunky to shift between text boxes and formatting commands. If I were to use the freeform pen, my lack of a stylus and pad makes anything I try to write or draw look like it was written by a sleepy three-year-old.

Early on, I instead used my word processor, with page thumbnails visible if I had to write a lot of things on the fly or prepared slideshows again with thumbnails visible. I tend to use the slides more now that I'm used to teaching online and can get ahead on my lesson planning.

For the times when I had to explain something off the cuff, I would prepare the aforementioned word processor to display a special, horizontally oriented document using larger size easy-to-read fonts, as well as colored backgrounds. I found with judicious use of line breaks and cut and paste, what I may have lost in flexibility on a digital whiteboard in terms of moving text boxes around I more than made up for by having thumbnails at my disposal telling me where certain things I had typed before still were.

When I finish my lesson and save that word processor document, I still have editable text, whereas Zoom's whiteboard will save everything as an image file.

I use my word processor everyday, so my knowledge of the functions makes it easier for me to work nimbly with what I want to display.

I often use my whiteboard, slides, and web browser all tiled one on top of the other with my FaceTime preview displayed next to them, and displayed to students using Zoom's **Share portion of screen** function (see Part VIII). I can easily switch what I'm showing the students just by switching which app is on top of the others by calling it from my Mac OS dock.

I also like to sometimes impress students with Apple's voice recognition when I speak directly into the word processor and have it transcribe what I say.

PART 11

POLLS

One of the great advantages of the digital classroom is its ability to gather and collate information both with and from our students in so many ways. Google Forms made it easy to take surveys, and LMSs like Moodle made short work of making and assigning quizzes and questionnaires.

So when I first started looking at Zoom's Polls system back in 2020, I was keen to find out what it could do. I have to say I was a little disappointed, as while it could do a rudimentary job, it was clunky and inflexible. But I'm glad to say that Zoom polls have progressed since then, and if you haven't looked at them for a while, I suggest you give them another chance as they're much easier to use than before.

11.1 ARE ZOOM POLLS STILL CLUNKY AND HARD TO USE?

I stopped using Zoom Polls shortly after I first tried them around mid-summer 2020. I found them more trouble than they were worth. They involved having to go to the website to write a poll. All polls had to be written before a meeting began, and they couldn't be edited or created anytime after. I didn't take a lot of polls in class, but if I did, I made do with the "Yes/No" buttons in enhanced reactions. If I needed more than that, I frankly found making a Google Form more intuitive. This was all kind of a shame because I knew that Zoom had its own polls and a reporting system that let you download the results from their website.

I took another look at Zoom's in-meeting polls as part of my research for this book, and I found that while they still require you to write and edit your polls on the website, they are more flexible now, and I've even found a way for you to be able to take polls that you wrote for one class and move them over to another class without too much fuss and certainly without a need to rewrite all the questions and answers.

There are still limits to the polls. Each meeting can have only 25 polls, and each poll can have only 10 questions. You can relaunch a poll during a meeting—say if some students came late to a class and you wanted to get their answers—but Zoom's poll reports system on the website will record only the latest results of any poll in a meeting, so all of your students will have to do the poll again.

11.2 WHY CAN'T I FIND THE ADD POLL BUTTON?

If you can't seem to find the **Add** button for polls at the bottom of the meeting details page where you thought it was before, you probably pushed the **Edit Meeting** button. If you see a blue **Save** button, click that, and you will return to the main meeting settings page where you will find the **Add Poll** button at the bottom of the page where it should be.

To avoid the situation where you can't see the button in future, just click the title of the meeting, not the **Edit** button. And none of this matters if you're looking for an **Add Poll** button because your friend told you to try them, but she forgot to tell you that you need a paid account to have polls enabled.

11.3 HOW DO I EDIT A POLL AFTER A MEETING HAS STARTED?

A big complaint I had with Zoom polls was that after I wrote a poll, I couldn't edit it once I had started the meeting; say I wanted to add another answer option or edit a typo I'd just noticed. This has changed. You can now edit a poll all the way up to the point just before you launch it. You still have to be the original meeting host to do so, however. Even if you were given host control during a meeting, you won't be able to edit any unlaunched polls if you are not using the account with which the polls were made.

If you do have original host control, click the **Polling** button in your meeting toolbar and look to the top right corner of the poll window that appears. You'll see an **Edit** button. You'll still be redirected to the website to do the editing, so that's still clunkier than being able to do it in the app interface, but hey, baby steps.

You'll immediately be greeted when you arrive on the website not with the poll you want to edit, but instead with the interface to add a new poll. If that's what you want, knock yourself out, but if you want to edit an existing poll, close that add poll interface window by clicking the **X** button on the top right, or click the **Cancel** button at the bottom.

Once that disappears, you should have in front of you the existing polls already attached to your meeting, and the buttons you need to edit or delete any of them. Make your changes, and don't forget to save. Upon returning to your meeting, you will find that the Zoom poll window has suddenly refreshed, and any changes you made to any of the polls will now have registered.

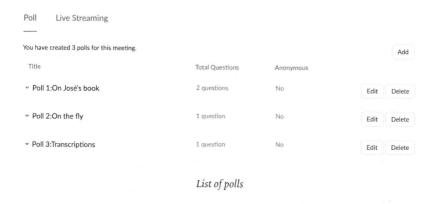

List of polls

If you have already launched a poll, it will not have any edit buttons but instead be labeled **Poll has ended**. At this point, all you can do is re-launch a poll back in the app interface, but there will be no way to edit it unless you relaunch the entire meeting. So before you launch an important poll, get into the habit of checking it over quickly before you hit the launch button.

Poll is ended

Edit   Delete

Edit   Delete

Options on a poll already launched

11.4 AFTER A MEETING/POLL, HOW CAN I SEE THE RESULTS?

You can see your poll results after your meeting by accessing your account on Zoom's website and clicking on **Reports** on the left-hand side.

You'll see two report types: **Usage** and **Meeting**. You might have a third option **Webinars** available. Click **Meeting**, and you'll get into Zoom's meeting report generator. There are two types of reports you can make, so make sure you choose **Poll Report**. The other one, **Registration Report**, only creates lists of individuals who attended your meeting.

Generate Poll Reports here

Once you choose **Poll Report**, enter the date ranges for the polls you want to see. As I live in Japan, if I am scheduling an international meeting, I play it safe by putting in dates that are a day before the time of the meeting to make sure that I can compensate for any time zone differences. Click the blue **Search** button, and you'll see the list of reports that fit in those dates. Choose the one you want by title, date, and start time. Generate the report, and it should automatically download to your computer.

If you can't seem to access your poll reports, it is possible that your account administrator has not allowed you access to poll report generation. If so, a quick phone call to their office asking for such access will probably do the trick. If you need access sooner than the time it takes your administrator to act, there is another way to access poll reports.

Click **Meetings** on your Zoom account's webpage and click the title of the relevant meeting. If your meeting just ended, you should have it listed immediately in front of you, and you can confirm it by looking at the date and time. If it happened a few hours in the past or more, click **Previous** meetings and it will be listed there.

Once you see the meeting details (If you mistakenly clicked to **Edit** the meeting, go back on your browser and click the meeting title instead), at the bottom of the page will be all the polls you created for that meeting. To the left of each poll title is a down arrow that you can click and it will reveal all the poll results. If you made a recurring meeting, however, any poll results will disappear as soon as you relaunch another instance of that recurring meeting.

11.5 HOW CAN I COPY THE POLLS I MADE FOR ONE CLASS TO ANOTHER CLASS?

Make the polls you want in the class you first want to use them in. They don't have to be perfect, as Zoom now has better on-the-fly editing capabilities for its polls than before.

Above the list of polls you made, you'll see an array of buttons. The one furthest to the right is **Save as Template**. Click that.

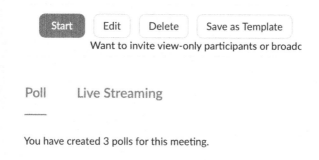

Save as template

Next, go back to the main meeting schedule in your Zoom website account. You'll find the template you just saved there if you click

Meeting Templates. Find your template by name and to the right of it is a button: **Use this Template**.

Click that to create a new version of the meeting you just saved. Edit the names and times and anything else you want to change. Then click the blue **Save** button. Go back to your list of meetings and you'll find your newly made meeting from the template.

Meeting Templates button on the far right.

Most importantly, check at the bottom and you'll find that your polls have all been copied over as well. You can keep that template as long as it suits you and toss it whenever you feel like it.

PART 12

ZOOM FOR OTHER
EDUCATIONAL
PURPOSES

For many of us, Zoom is so much a part of our teaching now that we sometimes forget that it's designed primarily as meeting software. Its ability to be adapted to different communication situations is good a witness to how well it was put together. Apart from classroom uses, here are some other ways that Zoom can work in education.

12.1 HOW IS ZOOM USED IN ACADEMIC CONFERENCES?

2020 was a memorable year for academics, pleasantly so or otherwise. Not only did teachers have to scramble for solutions to the need for a digital presence, but academic organizations had to move their conferences online as well; either that or they had to cancel them.

Almost all academic conferences that went online in Japan in 2020 were done on Zoom. I was privileged to be involved in organizing three online conferences: two for the Japan Association for Language Teaching and one for Online Teaching Japan.

My particular specialty in Zoom saw me being tasked with creating and implementing protocols for those conferences to use in moving all their keynotes, plenaries, seminars, and presentations online. The majority of my work was in writing those protocols and assembling and training the teams of volunteers at those events.

I couldn't have done it without Jennie Crittenden and Adam Jenkins. Along with Samantha Kawakami, Alexandra Burke, Phil Nguyen, and Mizuca Tsukamoto, we were known as the "Fire Station" for the JALT 2020 International Conference.

12.2 WHAT IS A CONFERENCE "ROOM HOST"?

Using Zoom in academic conferences is about making sure the presenter can deliver their content to the audience as seamlessly as possible. This requires the presence of a "room host," a designated conference team member who watches over the technical needs in the Zoom room for that particular presentation.

A good room host should be quite experienced in Zoom and able to quickly think on their feet—or in this case, their seat. Room hosts might be faced with problems such as presenters having trouble logging in, mixups in the scheduling, problems with the presenter's soft/hardware, or as in my case, sometimes even having to soothe the nerves of a nervous first-time presenter.

They should, nevertheless, be almost invisible to the audience. Of course, the host will still have to make announcements and give directions at certain times, but if all goes well, the audience will come away from the presentation remembering nothing about the room host because they were thinking so much about the presentation.

Thus, a conference setting highlights the importance of well-prepared staff. Some presenters, while experienced in online teaching, may have been using Webex or MS Teams exclusively. The room host will be managing their unfamiliarity with the software, the room timing, getting the questions from the audience to the presenter, distributing any associated documentation or links, and potential security intrusions.

At large conferences with over 50 presentations, those room hosts should be supported by a well-prepared team of troubleshooters who have the knowledge and experience to deal with more complicated problems that no one could have foreseen. One example is a presenter who thought they could do their presentation while they were on vacation, using the hotel wifi via their spouse's computer, which had never been used for Zoom before; good times, great memories.

A good conference will also pay attention to security issues. While it happened only twice, and only early on in my Zoom career, I have been Zoombombed before. Once it happened to me directly, and one other time in a presentation I was managing. Security in Zoom rooms is harder to completely lock down than one would imagine, but keeping links secure and having a robust login authentication system should be at the forefront of planning for conference organizers.

12.3 HOW CAN I USE ZOOM'S FUNCTION FOR SIMULTANEOUS INTERPRETATION?

Around the end of 2020, Zoom brought in a feature that allows a host to assign simultaneous interpretation duties to individual meeting participants. While they intended this as a way to facilitate communication in multilingual business meetings, I was imagining right away that this would be useful in academic conferences. Then I imagined that it might be useful for actual pedagogical situations as well.

The most obvious one is for teachers conducting interpretation classes. The teacher manages the interpreter settings as well as the screen sharing of the material to be shared and the recording of the session. The other students in the class are tasked with assessing the student doing the interpreting. Students take turns interpreting something such as a YouTube video the teacher prepared.

It might also be useful if you are a language teacher teaching a group of kids and their parents are visiting your Zoom class. You could have your assistant explaining to the parents in their native language about what you are doing while you are teaching. The teacher can't hear what is being said inside the interpretation channel, so it's not distracting.

The controls can be a bit fidgety, but they become less difficult to use with practice. Nonetheless, the students will need to be familiar with them well before an actual test happens. If you use this feature a few times during class for shorter assignments, the students should be familiar with it enough that come test time, and there shouldn't be many problems. Warn your students not to be connected to the Zoom classroom on just a phone when it's their turn to interpret.

Language Interpretation
Allow host to assign participants as interpreters who can interpret one language into another in real-time. Host can assign interpreters when scheduling or during the meeting.

9 languages +

English   Chinese   Japanese   German   French   Russian   Portuguese

Spanish   Korean

Default interpretation language choices

You need to enable the feature before you start using it, so look for **Language Interpretation** in your account's website settings. Here you can also add any other languages you want specified in the list. Click the plus button + above the array of languages to do that.

Almost everything else you need to do can be done during the meeting, except for adding at least one interpreter to the list of designated interpreters. That you have to do when you schedule the actual class.

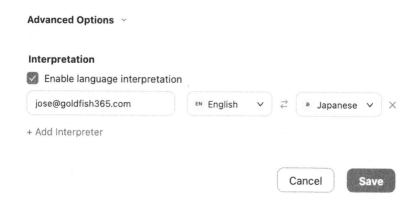

Adding a designated interpreter

If you're a teacher using this feature for your interpretation class, it doesn't really matter who is designated at this point, so you may as well just enter your own email. Remember, you can edit who will be interpreting fairly easily on the fly during the meeting.

Zoom has a pretty good support page explaining how to manage interpretation features. Give yourself plenty of time to try it out, however, as the controls are not always intuitive, and it's easy to forget at first that you might still have interpretation turned on or turned off when what you want is the opposite.

12.4 HOW CAN I BEST USE ZOOM FOR PRE-RECORDING PRESENTATIONS?

Zoom actually makes a great platform for recording a lesson. Many academic conferences have the option of submitting your presentation as a prerecorded video. Basically, you have at your disposal all the same screen-sharing functions that you have for classes, whether you are teaching an actual class or just making a meeting with only you in attendance. So prepare your presentation or asynchronous lesson, get ready to deliver it, and hit the record button.

Once you have the recording, trim the start and ends to take out any extraneous footage, and you're generally good to go.

One problem that occurs with recordings, however, is that normally the default size of your camera in the recording is much smaller than the recorded shared material. I go over this in the section on Zoom window management as well, but you can get Zoom to record a much larger image of your camera if during the share, you enlarge the active speaker video image by dragging its corner. I suggest you do a little test video so you can see if you like the effect.

When I do a prerecorded presentation, however, I don't like that my camera image is oriented horizontally next to the also horizontal shared material. When I enlarge my image it stretches the width of the video so far that it starts to look odd.

Instead, I like to use Zoom functions to achieve a look that I first started showing to other university instructors in Japan back at the beginning of the pandemic. You can see a sample of it in the screenshot. At the time of this writing, I can only achieve this on a Mac, but camera software might have changed for Windows or other platforms, so this may be possible there now as well.

Presenter video sized to match the screen size.

Basically, you are still doing the main recording in Zoom, but instead of sharing a window, you use the option to share a **Portion of Screen**. First, though, configure your material to be shared so that it is in about a 6:4 ratio. Then start your Mac's FaceTime software, which will start its camera preview, which is in a vertical orientation. This allows you to create a more natural-looking overall proportion in the resulting video, which should end up at 9:5.

Set the FaceTime video preview's contact listings underneath the material you want to show and open the **Portion of Screen** sharing option. Don't forget to click the **Share sound** and **Optimize for video clip** checkboxes. Position the green border indicating the share area to capture an image similar to the screenshot example in the previous image.

You should make sure that the **active speaker video** camera has been turned off by clicking the single bar at its top left.

Even after you have started sharing, you can start your recording by accessing the Sharing toolbar and clicking the **More** button on the extreme right.

Single flat bar when clicked collapses presenter video

Before you start recording, make sure you have nothing on top of the material you want to show, such as the Zoom sharing toolbar or the aforementioned active speaker video box. Since you already have your image in the FaceTime preview, you can turn off the video preview by turning off your camera in Zoom.

I make a few small edits to trim the start and end of the video as well as put in my logo in my video editing software. If you do a good job in your presentation entry and exit, you might not even need to do that.

12.5 HOW CAN I DELIVER A WEBINAR?

WHAT IS A WEBINAR?

Think of a large auditorium with a large audience in front of the stage. The event is being recorded, so there are studio-quality lights and cameras. As the presentation begins, several panelists are brought onto the stage and are introduced by the MC or lead presenter. The event then continues with most everyone participating, quietly watching the interplay on the stage from the darkened audience seats and hoping to get a chance to ask a question if the opportunity arrives.

So, if we can think of a Zoom virtual meeting as a classroom, the above is basically the parallel analogy to what a webinar is.

Webinars are designed to have large attendance figures and are designed for less interactivity between the stage panelists and the audience. There is still a room host who is the main room controller, but often this person is not immediately visible to the main audience. The audience will be able to see all the panelists speak to each other but generally cannot speak among themselves. This allows the host managing the webinar to control the environment better for questions and answers, polls, and room entry and exit.

IS IT POSSIBLE TO MIMIC A WEBINAR SETTING WITH A REGULAR ZOOM ACCOUNT?

Webinars are available as a paid add-on feature to an account, and are generally used for large events. They can be quite costly, so most teachers wouldn't be able to afford the feature for their classroom. But if you think you'd like to have something like a guest panel visible to a large-ish crowd of say, 80-90 people, there are ways to mimic what webinars do. (Remember that a regular account can only have a total of 100 people in it, although that number can be temporarily upgraded if you purchase the **Large Meeting** monthly plan from Zoom.)

When scheduling the meeting, set the security requirements for requiring participants to be muted and have their cameras turned off upon entry. I would also suggest that you follow my recommendations for meeting security, and to at least use the Zoom registration system in order to help confirm your audience identities and attendance numbers.

When the event begins, tell the audience to please keep their cameras off and that you will be strictly muting them to avoid any interruptions. Questions will be taken only in chat or after a hand has been raised in the meeting reactions.

To mimic the effect of having a series of guests visible at all times to each other and to the (mostly) quiet audience, you can use Zoom's "multi-spotlight" feature, which forces all participants into gallery view with all of the speakers the room host has spotlighted. Multi-spotlight is available in the participants list in each person's

More button. You can have up to nine people arranged in a multi spotlight. I've used this system fairly successfully in academic presentations that had multiple speakers. The added advantage is that individual audience members can turn their cameras on when asking questions.

12.6 HOW CAN I SEND LARGE ZOOM RECORDINGS TO THEIR DESTINATION?

After you have made your recording in Zoom and end the meeting, you'll find the resulting mp4 video file in the Zoom files folder, which is usually inside your computer's Documents folder, with each meeting in its own folder, labeled according to date and time.

If you made a recording, it'll be in the appropriate folder, labeled **zoom_0.mp4**. If you started and stopped the recording more than once during the meeting, you'll have more than one such file, and the newest recordings will have higher numbers.

Options for recording

If you will be editing your Zoom recordings, I suggest that you go to Application settings and in the **Recording** settings, find the checkbox for **Optimize for 3rd party video editor**. This will ensure that you get the highest quality recording possible.

You might be faced with a bit of a problem if your file is over the normal file size limit for email delivery. Most email accounts limit the email they allow to be delivered to attachments that total only about 50-100 megabytes. A video file will easily go over that after about 5-7 minutes of recording. If you edit the file with even a simple video editor, that can also enlarge the file.

If you have a paid account and you made a cloud recording, you'll find it on the Zoom website inside your account's **Recordings** page. To transfer large Zoom recordings, consider recording them to the cloud, so your recipient download them easily as soon as you send the download access link, and passcode if you set one. But doing that would mean that you wouldn't be able to edit it first, so make sure the video is ready before they download it by viewing it all the way through.

Otherwise, there are file-sharing alternatives such as Dropbox or MS OneDrive. I use my Google drive. Copy the file to either of those drive services, and share the link with the other party. Both Google Drive and MS OneDrive have complete instructions for sharing files.

You can also use online sites such as http://hightail.com and https://wetransfer.com to send large files. Both of these services have a free option and a paid option (for extremely large files).

12.7 HOW DOES ZOOM FIT INTO HYBRID/HYFLEX CLASSES?

Hybrid classes can refer to several different adjustments to a classroom schedule or setup. They were introduced by schools from K-12 to university to accommodate having some students in the classroom while others participate in a virtual space. The class teacher is sometimes asked to create dual syllabuses: one for those who attend the classroom, and one for those who stay home. Some schools have students split time, on a bi-weekly schedule, every other week in class, every other in the virtual space.

Still other schools use a "hyflex" model, where in every class session, the teacher has to handle students in both the virtual and physical space simultaneously. This can be quite challenging— making sure all students are engaged, designing tasks that all students can do together, answering questions coming from both directions, and then doing your best to assess all students fairly. One of the more generous descriptions I heard a teacher use to describe a hyflex situation was "exhausting"; a less generous one was "nightmare."

Actually, I think it's not really the hybrid/hyflex model that we dislike, it's being forced to implement it without enough time to properly train ourselves and adjust our teaching systems, and of course in some contexts, while worrying about a killer virus in the air.

There are advantages to the hybrid model for physically distant students; for example, students unable to come to class for health reasons or because they lack transportation. However, to be told to hold hybrid classes with little or no support from the institutions, not even improvement for wifi in the classrooms, creates trepidation among teachers.

Some university students, when asked what they didn't like about their education during the pandemic, noted that with the remote style or hybrid classes, they were forced to pay for classes that were not what they'd signed up for.

There is no model of hybrid classes that can be implemented successfully without preparation, without a stable and capable LMS, without wifi in the classrooms, without a proper assay of what students have at home in terms of connectivity and hardware availability. In some countries like Japan, digital literacy is not taught in most high schools.

However, remote learning can be quite successful when both instructors and students are prepared and motivated to engage remotely, so it is not necessarily the hybrid model that is the problem; it is the way that classrooms are being squeezed into it with little in the way of support and preparation.

It is very difficult to come up with any specific set of recommendations, especially for hyflex classrooms, as any recommendation is so dependent on the variables each school has laid down as directives, such as:

- how to handle social distancing
- how to plan for hybrid, bi-weekly schedules
- what kind of class is being taught: lecture-style or conference-style
- access to an LMS

The feasibility and potential success of anything we plan for a hyflex class is so dependent on all of these.

Still, it is obvious that the pandemic permanently changed the way we think of technology in our classrooms and perhaps how we think of education itself. By January of 2021, I had become so accustomed to my newly found digital skills that I am now looking for new ways to make my communication classes almost free of paper, even though all the way up to 2020 I thought of computers and phones as classroom distractions. Now I am adamant that if I do achieve a paperless classroom, it will be with the help of an LMS, something I have only seen on my horizon since I was forced into emergency remote teaching.

The emergency will be over eventually. The potential advantages of blended and hybrid education will not. Online education is already clearly a success, as it allows post-graduate programs to take advantage of new technologies to bring a stronger immediacy to their students over a distance. This is a godsend to certain students with special needs. MOOCs (Massive Open Online Courses) suddenly see new opportunities. On the other hand, without adequate support and training, teachers need to exert incredible amounts of effort to cope with not only hyflex teaching, which is work enough, but also doing it while trying to follow whatever other directives the school may have placed on them.

However, some teachers do get the training they need. Some schools have upgraded their campus wifi and the hardware for audio and video in the classrooms. The advice here is for the not-uncommon worst-case scenario of a teacher dealing with a school pulled to its own breaking point by the pandemic or otherwise is ill prepared, with no budget and inadequate support from the IT department.

I've had conversations with other teachers who are doing hybrid / hyflex classes in that nightmare scenario, and after even all that, I have a few pieces of advice to offer. I'm a gearhead, so of course the first one is about microphone setups.

12.8 WHAT SHOULD I DO ABOUT MY MICROPHONE IF I WANT TO LEAVE THE DESK IN A HYFLEX CLASS?

If you're in one of those really tough situations where you have to attend to students both in a virtual space in Zoom while simultaneously looking after students in front of you, consider this: depending on social distancing rules and your own penchant for moving around the room, you might have a need to be at a distance from your Zoom host computer.

Consider logging in with your smartphone into the Zoom room, along with the host computer. Use wired headphones or Bluetooth earbuds to get your voice via the phone into the Zoom room. This will allow you to hear what is happening in the virtual space even while you're walking around the classroom or if you've moved a little bit away from the lectern or desk. Smartphones will use energy quickly, so charge in between classes, and an external battery is recommended. The main host computer would be doing the heavy lifting of sharing screens and managing participant room entry, etc., which would be a pain to do on a phone.

Now here comes the hard part. You cannot have two separate devices in the same Zoom room if they're within audio pickup range of each other. If you do, you'll get an audio echo "howl." But if one of those devices disconnects audio from Zoom, they can coexist, and as long as they take turns connecting and reconnecting, they can both still participate throughout the meeting. They just can't have audio connected simultaneously.

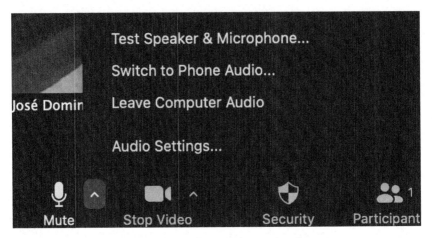

"Leave Computer Audio" on desktop version of Zoom

To **Disconnect Audio** means that neither the microphone nor the audio output device will work. On a computer in-meeting, that command is second from the bottom in the audio pop-up menu labeled **Leave Computer Audio**. On a mobile device, it's accessed from the in-meeting **More** menu and is marked in red letters, **Disconnect Audio**.

My suggestion is that both the computer on your physical classroom desk and your smartphone be logged into the same Zoom room, but that the computer's audio remain disconnected. That way you hear and can communicate with the students in the virtual space via your smartphone and its connected audio device.

If there is ever a need for the students in both the virtual space and the physical space to be able to communicate with each other en masse, a microphone can be set in the middle of the physical classroom and set so that any questions a physical student needs to ask can be heard by students in the virtual space. That microphone can be connected to the desk computer via USB, which would require the smartphone audio to be disconnected while the computer's audio is reconnected for those student questions. Once the physically present student asks a question, the computer can be disconnected from audio again, and you can reconnect on your smartphone.

As for any specific one-to-one student interactivity between students across the virtual and physical spaces, that will require more extensive hardware arrangements. Also remember that any devices being used simultaneously in the virtual and physical spaces cannot be in audio range of each other, so all students must be on headsets and should try to speak in lower voices if they're in the physical room together.

12.9 WHAT'S YOUR OTHER PIECE OF ADVICE FOR EMERGENCY HYFLEX CLASSES?

Let's imagine a scenario that is the worst of all cases: a need for the virtual space to communicate with the physical space; and a need for the teacher to move around inside the physical space away from a stationary microphone, far enough away that Bluetooth audio connectivity can't be maintained between the desk computer and the teachers headset. I'm imagining very little in terms of useful audio facilities in the room, and only one teacher to manage it all.

There are myriad possible solutions for each possible scenario depending on what audio / video / internet facilities are available —at which point you will need to adjust and experiment to find an operating procedure that might work for you.

So my second piece of advice is that not only in that case but throughout your hyflex teaching year, you stay flexible and sympathetic to your own situation as well as to your students'. It's a very difficult thing to be thrown into a hyflex class with inadequate equipment and preparation, and doing it while worrying about your own health is even harder still.

Try not to take too much of the difficulty of the day back home with you. Make sure to get your rest and chances to refresh your spirit. Sympathize and communicate with your students about what everyone—including you—is feeling about what makes this hard.

You will probably not be able to follow your curriculum as you initially planned it, so prepare for that. But through it all, remember that you are learning a new skill that could have great relevance going into the future even after the pandemic.

As discussed earlier, with good preparation and proper institutional support hyflex classes can be a boon for students who for one reason or another cannot attend a class. Some schools and parents are reporting anecdotally that their students and children are doing much better online than they were before in physical classes. (See https://www.kqed.org/mindshift/57480/as-many-parents-fret-over-remote-learning-some-find-their-kids-are-thriving?)

If you work it right, maybe you can be instrumental in taking what you've learned and helping your school establish a program for kids who stopped attending school, or help ease them back into the physical classroom step by step.

Look to what you can get out of this pile of lemons; I don't know, lemon cake? A glass half-full of lemonade?

12.10 WHAT IS ZOOM LIKE FOR SOCIAL EVENTS?

In the spring of 2020, I started running a weekly social gathering on Zoom for the members of the Facebook group Online Teaching Japan. Every Friday night since April 24, OTJ people and any others would come and join us to enjoy one another's company on Zoom and share and imbibe, confide and complain, and generally just have a chance to relax at the end of every week of teaching during the pandemic.

For many people, me included, it was a major part of that year's social occasions. And even though I thought at first it would be a one-off chance for the members of an asynchronous discussion group on Facebook to meet on Zoom, the response from everyone who attended was immediately to ask me for the URL for the gathering for next Friday. I made a lot of friends at what we came to know as the Friday Night Social (FNS), and I credit them with helping me keep a lighter heart and a bigger smile.

I suggest all associations, social or academic, loose-knit or traditional and highly organized, sponsor such socially distanced gatherings when physical distance is imposed. While it's true that many of us want to travel and see new things again, another crucial thing we miss is each other's company. And the quality of that company does not diminish very much over Zoom when it is between friends. Establishing this early on can create important social avenues for classes, organizations, or programs that span large territories and distances, too.

Schedule a recurring meeting so that the invitation will include an .ics file that people can put into their calendar software. Keep the atmosphere light and not too laden with shoptalk. Neckties and titles should be left outside the door.

The person who is running the room will have a bit more of a responsibility the first few times to keep an eye on things, especially when it comes to clashing views on politics, work habits, or potential points of friction. People have to know that while they can speak freely, inappropriate statements or behavior will be dealt with, so that all can come to trust the gathering as a place where they feel safe and able to relax even while engaging in lively conversations. This is the role of the room host: to watch over their colleagues until the room creates its own sustainable dynamic, running on the enthusiasm and energy of its own members.

With host control, you can make breakout rooms where people can be in smaller groups, allowing for more people to talk more often, instead of only one or two people only taking too much of the speaking time. The host should take note of when the women might be finding themselves fighting for speaking time. Yes, that happened to us at our OTJ FNS, and it could still quite easily happen again if we stopped watching for it. For the most part, however, judicious timing of breakout rooms can solve a fair amount of this, especially now that breakout rooms are user selectable; anyone can leave and go to any room they like whenever they want.

When making the breakout rooms, I rename them according to themes that pop up in the prior conversations, and if no such themes come to mind, I ask the audience for suggestions, or just choose anything that seems humorous and liable to spark a knowing smile or a laugh.

I suggest setting the breakout rooms to 30 minutes at a time, and starting them when you have about 10-12 people gathered. No matter how many rooms you set up, make two or three extra rooms that remain unnamed, so that if two people wish to discuss something with a little more privacy, they can go to one of the undesignated rooms to discuss it there. Thirty minutes might seem like a long time, but trust me, it's not, because people are free to move around the rooms as they like and will remain where they want to be.

After one set of rooms is done, everyone can gather in the main room again for a few minutes and enjoy the company of the whole group for a bit and maybe bring up some new topics. The room host can take this time to think of new room topics, and members might take the opportunity to bring up a discussion question for everyone to think about.

In my advanced years, I don't always like to stay up as late as some of the group's die-hards do every week. When it's time for me to sign off, I negotiate with the next person to whom I will pass host control, go brush my teeth, and retire for the night, happy to have had a chance to talk with good friends yet again.

PRO TIP: You know how it's always so awkward to say goodbye in Zoom because sometimes you just said your really heartfelt goodbye, and then you have to spend a few seconds with a goofy look on your face because you have to fumble with pointing your cursor for both the **Leave** *button and then have to confirm it with the second button? I suggest you time your goodbye so when you absolutely know you will* *say your final goodbye, click **Leave** first. From there, the confirming **End** (**Leave** for non-hosts) button can be activated anytime you hit your return key. This lets you say goodbye while you're actually still waving and looking into the camera.*

12.11 DOES ZOOM HAVE A REGISTRATION SYSTEM FOR SPECIAL EVENTS?

Yes, it does. Scheduling a special event can entail a few more concerns about controlling who is attending. Even if you set all of the security protocols for your meetings, it can be handy to know who is coming. It also helps build up your user email list; make sure you ask for permission to add people to that list, however.

To enable Zoom's event registration function, you have to schedule your meeting on the website, not in the Zoom application.

When you schedule a meeting, you'll find a checkbox to enable **Registration** just above the Meeting ID radio buttons. Check that and set your meeting details as you like.

Registration   ☑ **Required**

Meeting ID   ⊙ **Generate Automatically**

Checking "Required" turns on registration

Once you save the meeting, it will appear in the meeting list like other meetings, but if you look carefully once the page refreshes, after you save the meeting, a **Registration** link will be where the direct link to most meetings is. If you hand that out, your users will land on the registration page where they fill in their information.

Meeting Registration

This meeting is for users with a Zoom account. New to Zoom? Sign up free.

Topic	Registration required
Time	Mar 30, 2021 07:00 PM in Osaka, Sapporo, Tokyo

First Name*

Last Name*

Email Address*

Confirm Email Address*

* Required information

Register

The meeting registration form

Once they send that information, the page will refresh with confirmation of their registration and a link they can click to join the meeting. They'll also receive an email with the same information.

PART 13

MISCELLANEOUS

13.1 WHAT CAN I DO TO AVOID ZOOM FATIGUE?

Zoom fatigue has become such a common term that we have come to connect Zoom with yet another negative aspect of online education. Certainly I know the tired eyes, headaches, and generally taxed feeling that come from teaching three or four classes in one day, all of them over Zoom or some other similar teleconferencing software like Webex or Microsoft Teams.

Much of it is not actually a unique result only from using the software. For example, sitting in an office chair for long periods of time has been known to be a big problem for office workers for some time now. Yet this last year, I have referred semi-affectionately to "Zoom butt," and my fellow teachers all know exactly what I'm talking about. I almost always stand up in my normal classrooms, and it felt quite strange having to sit down in a chair to teach.

We can alleviate a lot of the problems we consider to be Zoom fatigue by following some simple procedures known to be effective for those who work long hours at a computer: short stretching or walking breaks scheduled throughout the day.

If your students are in breakout rooms, or when class is over, use the opportunity to look out the window and focus your eyes on a distant building or mountain while you sip your tea.

If your hands are bothering you from too much mousing, there are several internet sites that will teach you how to avoid repetitive stress syndrome. I for one long ago learned how to be ambidextrous when it comes to working on my Mac, both on a trackpad or a mouse. Switching between hands and devices can give one set of muscles enough of a break that they don't get injured, while not necessitating any downtime in your teaching schedule.

An issue that contributes to eye fatigue from sitting down in front a computer is the need to look at white text pages, light-colored web sites, and basically a lot of small dark text on light backgrounds. On small computer screens, the problem is that the text gets smaller; on bigger computer monitors, the problem is compounded by having so much light coming from a bigger source.

To counter this, I cannot recommend enough that you begin using your computer in dark mode. This is a setting that will make your monitor work with darker colors, and as much as possible, light text on black backgrounds. I felt much less eyestrain when I started using dark mode on my social media sites, and on as many other websites as possible.

To do this yourself, search for the words "dark mode" in the help sections for your computer, and the software and websites you use. Facebook has an excellent dark mode setting, and many Moodle sites can be configured to display in dark mode with a couple of button clicks. Zoom has its own dark node setting in the application settings. See more about this in section 6.2.

So when people talk about Zoom fatigue, I wonder how much the nature of the problem is actually just those ergonomic issues. I hope they try to take a few careful steps to alleviate or prevent them.

Moreover, while I would agree with those who would say that their Zoom fatigue increases the more they use the software, I have also for the past year been attending a weekly social get together for a group of teachers every Friday night. We've been coming together sometimes to talk shop, but mostly just to enjoy one another's company. I usually leave around midnight, while others often stay much later, but by the time I'm done I will have been sitting there talking and drinking with friends for four hours or so, and in that length of time, I feel no more or less fatigue than I would have if I were enjoying good company in person.

13.2 ARE YOU SAYING THAT ZOOM FATIGUE ISN'T ACTUALLY A THING?

I think the idea of Zoom fatigue might be arising out of causes that are unique to trying to communicate to or with others in ways to which we are not accustomed. As educators we have honed skills for reading a room of students. We can tell by looking across an audience if the students are eager or not, puzzled or not. In addition, we can also tell when sitting face to face with one student or a small group how our messages are being received.

Working during a quarantine or in an online environment makes that so much more difficult. Research on face-to-face communication shows that we subconsciously take cues from one another's micro expressions to perform those assessments of our audience that I mentioned earlier.

Part of what makes us "fatigued" is our brain working overtime trying, as both students and teachers, to understand not just the content but the people in that Zoom room, all of it unfamiliar to us.

My friend Curtis Hart Kelly, an expert in the connection between brain research and linguistics, says that we should pay good attention to the social needs of our students while we continue to teach. Doing so will probably benefit not only them but ourselves. We weren't used to doing that on video, and that caused us and our students extra stress. However, over time, I've noticed the task getting easier and easier for me, as I adjust to learning how to read faces in a different way. Not too oddly, it reminded me of the stress I feel whenever I start teaching at a different school, or when I went from teaching at conversation schools to teaching at university.

Talking to my friends on Friday nights produces little if any fatigue, as I know these people, and I know their voices without even seeing their faces. Over the year we've even created little micro-cultural norms of how we behave in the social event. In a class-room, it's hard to establish that; even harder in a class of anxious students. For teachers, our fatigue might be coming from trying to balance our lesson delivery with students who are only two-dimensional avatars of themselves. Instead of seeing them happy at being able to meet their friends, they are looking a little confused, operating software and hardware they don't know yet.

Thus I am not entirely convinced that Zoom creates a unique kind of unavoidable fatigue that automatically increases as you spend time using it. Alex Lindsay addressed this in a Medium blog post. He made an excellent analogy: anyone being taken from a tropical resort dressed for an afternoon on the beach and teleported to a ski hill would complain and probably not enjoy themselves very much. But is that because a weekend in a Swiss ski lodge is such a horrible place, or is it because anyone not prepared and outfitted properly would not enjoy the experience? How long would it take until our confused sunbather gets around to mastering the hills and comes to appreciate the differences in the situation?

Many educators here in Japan used the term Emergency Remote Teaching (ERT) for the 2020 academic year, to describe how both teachers and students had to very quickly adapt to a situation for which few of us were prepared. My friend Adam Jenkins, however, prefers to use his own term, Reduced/Altered Toolset Teaching (RATT). Adam is a system administrator and an expert in the Moodle LMS. Naturally he is quite adept at most tools related to online teaching. To him and his EdTech-proficient peers, Zoom is no more than a tool, and like a hammer it can be swung skillfully, or you can end up with a sore thumb.

I think a lot of what educators identify as "Zoom fatigue" was related to the burden we felt having to suddenly adjust to new tools, and not being able to teach in ways we prefer or were familiar with. We were receiving confusing directives from our schools, and sometimes little in the way of support. This was reinforced by the difficulty of teaching students who themselves perhaps did not want to study from a computer.

Teachers I know who both taught and were taught over videoconferencing systems before the pandemic tell me that the experience overall was no better or worse than any done in traditional teaching environments. The teachers were prepared, the students knew what they were in for, and everyone worked hard; with all that, any educational situation can be successful, and the stress it produces and the energy it requires shouldn't be much different from what we have always encountered as educators.

13.3 IS THERE ANYTHING I SHOULD NOTE ABOUT THE VIEW BUTTON?

Not much, except that as part of what teachers can do to encourage students to turn on their cameras, one small thing that might help is to actually take the time to show all your students that Zoom allows them to see everyone's cameras. I generally encourage my students to use Gallery view. To do that more easily, see the question after this on the meeting toolbar, about **Show Zoom windows during screen share**.

Other teachers go the opposite route and insist that they spotlight themselves throughout the lesson. I don't know about you, but I would start to get tired of only being able to see one face in every class every week. I prefer gallery view in all my meetings, and I imagine most students would, too. Of course if you have to show materials or a slideshow, that's a different matter.

The View button is now where you access **Immersive View**, which you can read about in section 13.4.

13.4 WHAT IS IMMERSIVE VIEW?

In 2021, ZOOM released Immersive View (IV), which works from any computer that uses Mac OS or Windows running Zoom v5.6.3 or better. It takes the cameras of the host and participants and places them all in a virtual setting resembling a classroom or a café counter. Zoom engages a similar system to its virtual background to cut out the participants' silhouette from their background to make the effect a little more complete.

One of the immersive view options

In that first screenshot, you can see me and my friend Mike Lyons placed in a virtual café.

In the next screenshot, you can see the other virtual settings available, like a museum exhibit or an auditorium. At the bottom corner of each scene is a number indicating the maximum number of participants that can be set in the scene.

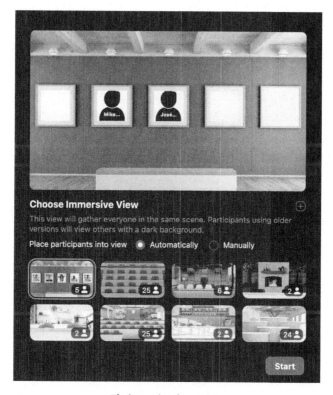

The immersive view options

To start IV, you need to go to your website settings to make sure the new feature is turned on. Then restart Zoom and log in. Start a meeting, and you will find that now under the normal choices for **Speaker** and **Gallery,** which appear when you click the **View** button, there will be a third choice, **Immersive View.** Click that, and most of the procedure will be fairly intuitive.

Immersive View

Allow hosts to curate case-specific scenes, such as a classroom or boardroom for their meetings or webinars.

Each scene allows you to move participants from chair to chair, and depending on the scene, you can sometimes also alter the size of each person's image. If a participant enters a room where the host has already engaged immersive view, they will appear outside of the immersive scene at the top of Zoom window. The host can easily place them into the scene by dragging their camera image into any vacant spot in the scene.

At first, you might think, IV is a nice idea, but does it have any pedagogical value? I think with a little imagination it's easy to think of at least a few places where it could be useful. There is one immersive scene that resembles a classroom where up to 25 students sit around a main speaker who's in a central position near the bottom of the view. This could be used for show and tell in a primary classroom, where the teacher places students in turns in the teacher's spot to do their talk. University students could do their semester presentations there.

IV only works in the main room, not in breakout rooms, but if students working on a group presentation can confer in breakout rooms before their group's turn to present, this might actually be good for creating some "facilitative anxiety" that culminates in them being placed on a special stage, a level above their normal practice room.

The 'art gallery' immersive scene

Other uses could involve the host engaging the option where they use their own camera as the immersive scene, in which the participants are placed to comment on what they see, such as the teacher's guitar playing technique or the execution of a magic trick. You can also upload images you take yourself to use as IVs, such as your own classroom or another place that is familiar or interesting to your students.

Only hosts can control the immersive view experience for the entire meeting, but another participant can be given this ability simply by giving them host control.

Finally, note that as of Zoom v5.6.4, Immersive View is not properly made part of any recordings you make. The Immersive background is either rendered a simple white background, or more likely, simply not recorded at all, and the video is simply in Gallery view. I would imagine Zoom is working on changing that, though.

13.5 WHAT'S INSIDE THE GREEN SHIELD BUTTON IN THE TOP RIGHT CORNER?

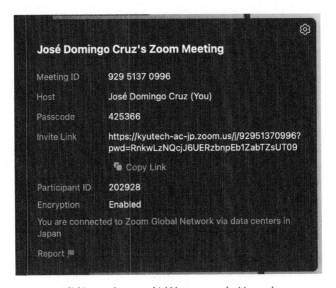

Clicking on the green shield button reveals this panel.

You'll find important information pertaining to the meeting identity and access information. If a trusted individual requests it, I can copy the meeting ID and password and paste them into a text chat window to send it to them (perhaps for them to pass on to a peer who can't access their email), via a screenshot. You might need to send a screenshot if the person trying to join didn't wait for you to send the link and went ahead and clicked the **Join** button on the main Zoom window. There they will get asked for Meeting IDs and Meeting passwords. Usually, though, I only need to click the button for "Copy Link" and send that.

Connecting by entering the meeting ID

PRO TIP: Upon starting a meeting, Zoom will automatically put the meeting URL in the clipboard ready for you to paste into a chat box. As soon as you see the message that it has done so in the meeting window, you are ready to pass along the URL. The message usually appears in the first few seconds.

13.6 WHAT ARE THE ADVANTAGES OF USING A LEARNING MANAGEMENT SYSTEM?

As this is a book about Zoom, I won't dwell too long on what a well-run Learning Management System (LMS) can bring to the table in terms of services to your class. But having a LMS handle your document distribution, distribute and manage your quizzes, perform your surveys, and even calculate your students' grades is almost incalculably better than just trying to use email or spreadsheets. Facebook social learning groups can act as a quasi-LMS, and even Zoom's own Channels functions can at least help you distribute files to members of a channel (group) faster and more efficiently than email ever will. An LMS is practically indispensable in distance education.

There are LMSs such as Edmodo that you can use as a paid service. Others still are tied to large platforms such as Microsoft Teams, Cisco Webex, or Google Classrooms. The best one will first be the one that your institution now uses. Schools will have at their disposal different LMSs depending on what they've contracted for. The universities where I work have services from Microsoft and Zoom. Others have Universal Passport or sometimes an in-house solution. Many others use the very popular open source LMS called Moodle, which is my overall recommendation.

As it is open source, Moodle is basically free software. Anyone can download and set it up on a server of their choice. That's not to say administering it is very easy. To maintain a good, fast, secure Moodle installation requires expertise in that area, but it is not impossible to learn how or even hire help to do it. Still, the software package itself is free, and so are all of its many upgrades and most of its very useful plugins. Your budget as a school owner who wanted to set it up could be focused on getting a good, fast server and hiring a skilled administrator. Searching in the internet under *Moodle Partners* should get you started.

13.7 HOW CAN I IMPROVE ACCESSIBILITY IN MY ZOOM CLASSES?

I have a friend named Alexandra Burke who has made quite a name for herself in EFL teaching circles in Japan. She's famous in this country for her crusade to bring more accessibility for students with neurodiversity issues such as ADHD, dyslexia, or dysgraphia. Her presentations have won awards for their value, and she's helped me figure out some of the most important things we as teachers need to know when it comes to helping the neurodiverse in our Zoom classes. The next few paragraphs will not at all be comprehensive, but they should point you in the right direction to bring in some easy-to-make changes to your Zoom teaching.

DOES MY MICROPHONE QUALITY AFFECT ACCESSIBILITY?

Absolutely. If you need another reason to take steps improve your Zoom audio quality, consider that students can go completely undiagnosed and live a life never knowing they have a hearing impairment. See Part IV: The Equipment Issue to improve your audio to make it easier for all of your students to hear you.

Also consider that not only in hybrid and hyflex classes should you be using a microphone in class. The statistical probability that students with hearing impairments will be attending our classes is the same in face-to-face classes as in online ones. You could think, *Then why don't they just move closer to the front?*, but I'm sure you realize that students sit at the back as much for reasons of peer pressure and culture as anything to do with their education.

WHAT SHOULD I CONSIDER WHEN CHOOSING COLORS AND FONTS IN MY SLIDES?

Just as Zoom itself has put in dark mode options for its interface, consider that you might want to do the same for your slides. With Alexandra Burke's help, all of my new slideshows for my presentations now use a dark green, mock-chalkboard background. The fonts I use are as large as the screen space allows. The text is white to contrast with the background, and highlight colors for things like arrows or shapes are in yellow. Avoid using red or blue on a green background for anything, because for students with certain types of color vision issues, those colors can be almost impossible to see. A black background with white text might appear to be better in terms of color contrast, but Alex recommended a mock chalkboard background, as it is a familiar for students coming out of a physical classroom and less intense in terms of absolute contrast as black and white might be. If you want to use typeface styles for emphasis, use bold, not underline or italics, as they reduce visibility.

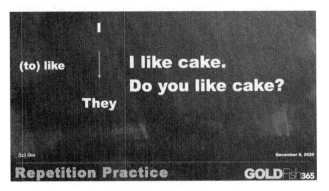

A dyslexic-friendly slide

There are certain on-screen fonts that are easier for dyslexic or other neurodiverse students to read and none of them are serif fonts. Stop using serif fonts. Increase the spacing in your lettering to about 1.3 and increase the leading to about 1.2. Use fonts in the family of "OpenDyslexic," which have been designed for students with that neurodiversity issue to more easily read the text. Consider using them everywhere—your handouts, your LMS font, your presentation slides.

CAN YOU POINT ME TO SOME NEURODIVERSITY RESOURCES?

Here's a quick list of resources you can access on the internet.

Alexandra Burke on neurodiversity.
https://jalt-publications.org/sites/default/files/pdf-article/44.3-tlt-yl.pdf

Statistics and clinical definitions of the different neurological conditions that can affect learning. This page covers design issues for autistic spectrum, screen readers, low vision, physical or motor disabilities, deaf or hard of hearing, and dyslexia, https://www.frontiersin.org/articles/10.3389/fnins.2016.00324/full

Designing for accessibility
https://accessibility.blog.gov.uk/2016/09/02/dos-and-donts-on-designing-for-accessibility/

British Dyslexia Association Dyslexia Style Guide.
https://www.bdadyslexia.org.uk/advice/employers/creating-a-dyslexia-friendly-workplace/dyslexia-friendly-style-guide

Many thanks, Alex. Keep up the good fight.

13.8 EXTERNAL RESOURCES

Here are a few places to go for more information.

OTJ AND THE RECORDINGS OF THE SUMMER SESSIONS

Throughout the time that I've been teaching with Zoom, that part of my career has been inextricably intertwined with an online support group on Facebook called "Online Teaching Japan" (OTJ) https://www.facebook.com/groups/603548090241536.

I very much would not be where I am right now if it weren't for the things that I learned there, the people I've met, and the events I've attended. The group is vibrantly active and well managed by the administrator and moderator, David Juteau and Cassie Guevara. Members are respectful and welcoming and some of the best teachers you will find from all levels of education in Japan. I cannot recommend it enough. I want to say thank you to everyone there for giving me the opportunities to become a better a teacher.

Part of the information that OTJ generated since 2020 is an event I had the privilege to be involved in called "The OTJ Summer

Sessions," a weeklong collection of member-produced talks, workshops, and seminars. These professional development events were recorded and made available for public reference. It's a great wealth of knowledge on what teachers were learning from the new world of emergency remote teaching and how they helped each other through it.

https://onlineteachingjapan.com/summer-sessions-calendar/

ZOOM RESOURCE AND SUPPORT PAGES

I've mentioned them before, but it bears emphasizing that Zoom has excellent **Resources** and **Support** pages on its website. The links are on the top right above your profile picture.

The **Resources** page is where you point students to download the latest version of the software, find Zoom-sponsored webinars, and video tutorials. In **Support** is an extensive database of information on Zoom features and solutions to problems. This will be important in the coming months as Zoom extends and evolves its software, bringing in new features that couldn't be discussed in this book.

CONCLUSION

2020 and 2021 were landmark years in the professional development of many teachers. We learned so much not just about Zoom and other digital tools, we also came to see ourselves and what education means to us in a different light.

Recordings of our lessons let us see more of ourselves as our students see us.

The problems that were thrown at us taught us where our limits were, and most of us found out that we were capable of much more than we thought.

Don't let your progress and momentum turn to complacency and inertia. Keep looking to improve yourself. Seek out communities like OTJ. It's hard to overestimate the importance of having a good circle of peers, family, and friends. When the Covid-19 pandemic is finally over, I hope it becomes clear how that protecting our mental health should be considered as normal and important as caring for our physical health. That point is made obvious by what was taken from us by our isolation in quarantine: the people who help us and whom we hold dear.

Even after the pandemic is over, you might find yourself in a situation where you are working on your own more often than you were before. As part of establishing a new lifestyle where remote teaching is a big part of what you do, make sure that you attend to the very important need to have others to talk to, both inside and outside of work. Stay in touch with the people you love. If you need to, find new social and professional discussion circles on social media.

In October 2020, Zoom outlined how their own research shows working from home didn't see the drop in worker productivity some companies feared, but worker mental health became a real problem. We have new educational opportunities brought to us by the new tools we have come to learn, but let's remember that it is still about people: our students and ourselves.

ACKNOWLEDGMENTS

I've never written a book before. I'm still amazed that I had an opportunity to write this one. One year ago I was just another teacher trying to figure out what to do for my remote classes.

But with the support and encouragement from so many people, here I am with the manuscript waiting to go to print and wondering to whom I need to show the deep gratitude I feel. There were a lot of people who made this possible, and I don't want anyone to think that they were noted less than anyone else by the order of their mention, so I'm going to say thank you in chronological order of their impact on the journey for this book.

First I want to thank "The Ladies." In the days just after Japan was in a panic about the new world the virus threw us all into, this group of students who let me experiment on techniques and methods with them started me on my learning on how to use Zoom. Ayano, Chiyomi, Nina, and Shiina—thank you so much, ladies. You helped me so much.

Thank you to my friend Steve Paton for giving me a chance to further hone my Zoom skills at the Fukuoka JALT meetings. Steve was the first person to say my name and the words "Zoom expert" in the same sentence.

I cannot say enough about the online group that supported and encouraged me as I wrote this book. I'm an English teacher, so I know how the word "literally" is overused. But I literally wouldn't have been able to write this book if I weren't a member of Online Teaching Japan (OTJ). Thank you to David Juteau and Cassie Guevara and all the wonderful, passionate teachers of OTJ that make me want to help; and especially to Dorothy Zemach who believed in me enough to give me this chance.

Also a big thank you to Joan Lambert Bailey, Richard Bailey, and Melodie Cook for helping with the proofreading.

And to a special core of friends that I was privileged to be part of, the "Fire Station": Alexandra "Alex the Awesome" Burke, Jennie "The Fire Chief" Crittenden, Adam "Leroy" Jenkins, Samantha "The Operator" Kawakami, Phil "CenCom" Nguyen, and Mizuca "The Cavalry" Tsukamoto. You guys are the best.

Finally, to my family back home in Canada: I miss you and love you all so much. Thank you for everything. And to my best friend Alexandre Costy: wetsuits and pushups forever, buddy. :)

JDC ("Firebug Snail")